WHERE'S MY MONEY?

10 SURE-FIRE WAYS TO
KEEP, EARN AND GROW MORE MONEY

JASON CUNNINGHAM

Wrightbooks

First published 2009 by Wrightbooks
an imprint of John Wiley & Sons Australia, Ltd
42 McDougall Street, Milton Qld 4064

Office also in Melbourne

Typeset in Berkeley LT 11.3/13.8pt

© Jason Cunningham 2009

The moral rights of the author have been asserted

National Library of Australia Cataloguing-in-Publication entry:

Author:	Cunningham, Jason.
Title:	Where's my money? / Jason Cunningham.
ISBN:	9780731408337 (pbk.)
Notes:	Includes index.
Subjects:	Finance, Personal.
	Corporations — Finance.
Dewey Number:	332.024

Front cover author photo © Karla Majnaric

Back cover author photo © Les O'Rourke

Printed in China by Printplus Limited

10 9 8 7 6 5 4 3 2 1

Disclaimer
The material in this publication is of the nature of general comment only, and does not represent professional advice. It is not intended to provide specific guidance for particular circumstances and it should not be relied on as the basis for any decision to take action or not take action on any matter which it covers. Readers should obtain professional advice where appropriate, before making any such decision. To the maximum extent permitted by law, the author and publisher disclaim all responsibility and liability to any person, arising directly or indirectly from any person taking or not taking action based upon the information in this publication.

Contents

To the three people who make me feel like I'm the most important person in their lives — Lewis, Jack and Tom.
Your Dad loves you very much.

Foreword

Passion and enthusiasm are words essential to playing elite sport, but are not necessarily associated with accounting—or accountants. I met Jason Cunningham through a mutual friend and I'd never met anyone with more energy and excitement towards everything he was associated with. I was in financial ruin and turning to Jason was my last chance. I thought there was no way out for me. After a brief meeting I left his office feeling on top of the world and believing that everything was going to turn out fine. After years of struggle I had finally met someone who could relate to me and my position, and who could instil the belief I needed to move forward. He didn't complicate things, he spoke in my language and he gave me hope when I thought there wasn't any.

As time passed we untangled the mess I had created and got to a stage where I was back in control. Throughout the process Jason and I became very good friends, and we still have a professional association. I never understood or learned about money while playing football—unfortunately it wasn't until after I'd retired that we met. That meeting changed my life (and my family's) forever. He is not only the very best in his field, he is also the very best of people. I have no hesitation in saying he's the best coach I've ever had.

Jason's unique qualities are evident throughout this fantastic book. He conveys a range of financial concepts in simple, straightforward language, and his passion, energy and personality shine through on every page. Most importantly, he provides the hope and encouragement needed—backed up by a step-by-step action plan—to make your dreams a reality.

David Schwarz
AFL commentator and
former Melbourne Football Club star

About the author

There are two distinct sides to Jason Cunningham. He's a mild-mannered accountant and partner in a successful accounting and advisory firm who also happens to be one of only seven accountants worldwide with a sense of humour. Reared on the mean streets of Pascoe Vale in Melbourne, there's an element of educated larrikin, raconteur and natural showman in Jason that enables him to relate to and inspire his clients. He talks straight and calls it as he sees it. Above all, he's passionate about helping people achieve their full financial potential.

CPA qualified, Jason completed his accounting degree with distinction. He's also a qualified financial planner with an Advanced Diploma of Financial Services (Financial Planning) and holds a financial planning licence.

In 1997 Jason co-founded an inner-city firm, The Practice, which provides accounting, taxation, business consulting, financial planning and finance solutions to a wide range of clients. From humble beginnings—just like the man himself—The Practice has grown from a staff of two (Jason and his business partner) to 25, with a turnover of $4 million. In 2007 The Practice won the inaugural Victorian Small Business Champion Award.

Jason has extensive experience in helping clients—from individual wage-earners, small business owners, executives and CEOs to publicly listed companies—grow and manage their financial affairs. A crucial part of his role is to help them identify and understand their needs and objectives, and give them the tools to reach their financial goals.

Jason has been recognised by CPA Australia as one of its premier trainers, and has presented and facilitated over 100 seminars and workshops for CPA members. He is chairperson of CPA's Public Practice Committee (Victorian Division).

Jason's specialty is the complex world of trading and tax. He has run numerous workshops and seminars for various share and option trading groups, and is considered an expert on the tax implications of trading the stock market. So much so, he was commissioned by two of Australia's top traders, Chris Tate and Louise Bedford, to prepare an audio program titled Trading and Tax. This hour-long dialogue, written and narrated by Jason, has proven extremely popular in trading and investing circles. Jason is also a regular presenter at the Traders and Investors Expo.

Acknowledgements

First and foremost, I want to thank a guy who without his help this book would not have been written. Brendan Keogh, you are a gun and a genius and no other person would have been able to articulate my spoken word into such a well-written book. Well done, mate—great achievement.

To the team at John Wiley & Sons—in particular, Kristen Hammond—thanks for asking me to have a crack at this and breaking me the whole way through the process.

Mum and Dad, I love you both very much. You guys have been the best parents I could have asked for. The lessons you have taught me throughout my life are the cornerstone on which this book was written. (Could you please update the will now?)

To the man known as The Ox, David Schwarz, thanks for those kind words in the foreword, they mean a lot to me. It was an honour to read such words of inspiration and then to realise they were written about me. Are you sure you were speaking about the right guy?

To Chris Tate and Louise Bedford, not only are you the best share traders in the Southern Hemisphere, but you are two wonderful people and great friends. Thanks for your contributions in chapter 9.

To my three case studies, thanks for agreeing to share your stories. There's a little bit of you in all of us.

Thanks to Karla for the great photography work—could have done a bit more with the air-brushing... Ah well, we'll leave that to book number two.

To my team at The Practice, one of the best things about our business is you guys. I know we have the best culture anyone could ask for and I really do enjoy coming to work every day. Thank you for supporting me during the time of writing and showing a genuine interest in how I've been progressing.

To my clients, thanks for teaching me everything you have. Oh, by the way, now that I'm a published author I just got 20 per cent more expensive.

To my wife, Ange, I love you belle. Thanks for putting up with a lunatic like me, I don't know how you do it. Well, yes, I do—it's called Tiffany's.

Introduction

Don't be fooled by the suave picture on the cover—underneath this debonair exterior, I'm just a humble bloke from the suburbs trying to earn a dollar and raise a family. Like most people, I've grappled with how to achieve that all-important balance in life: having enough money to be financially secure (with a little left over to enjoy the finer things in life from time to time), while not working so hard that life passes you by and leaves you with a no-expenses-spared funeral. Thankfully, my education and early years taught me the secret to achieving this: work *smarter*, not harder.

My own financial journey began with my upbringing and early jobs. Thanks to my parents, I learned the importance of money and hard work from an early age, and was fortunate to have great role models and mentors in my formative years. This book is for those of you who weren't so lucky.

Giving advice to clients all day, every day, has shown me that everyone makes the same financial mistakes—regardless of whether you're a battler or a brain surgeon. Sure, there are plenty of financial self-help books out there, but they're either not being read or not getting the message across. So I thought I'd put my pen where my mouth is (not *My Left Foot*–style — it's just a figure of speech) and write down my own philosophies in the hope it would help someone turn their fortunes around.

I'm passionate about helping people realise their potential. Some of my greatest business achievements have come from working with young people mired in debt or small business owners who feel swamped and helpless. I genuinely get excited about seeing the transformation in people who go from 'I can't see a way out' to 'I can do this'.

The principles and techniques I discuss in this book have been gathered, developed and refined over many years. I've reached them by observing my parents, colleagues and clients, building a successful small business, reading respected experts and through my own journey of self-discovery.

I also believe that the best way to learn is to become a teacher — so that's what I did. Presenting workshops to CPAs was a daunting challenge, but it motivated me to learn as much as I could about the subject matter and become an expert in that field in the process.

The examples, lessons and tips I provide are real, and they're easy to implement in your own life. No, you don't have to renounce everything, don a robe, move to a monastery and live on bread and water. I don't ask my clients to do anything I wouldn't do.

You work hard, with many more years ahead of you — who doesn't want to have something to show for it? I genuinely believe *everyone* can achieve financial prosperity. Just because you're not from a wealthy family doesn't mean you can't get on the money train. I'm living proof.

This book covers a range of topics, from basic financial concepts and my own philosophies to fairly full-on investment strategies. There's something for everyone — whether you earn $35 000 or $350 000.

I suggest that, even if you're reasonably financially astute, you use the early chapters as a refresher course on some of these concepts. It's important that we're both on the same page from the start, as I will regularly refer back to concepts covered in earlier chapters.

Like all great books, the best bit is the dramatic climax. In the final chapter I condense the key actions outlined throughout the book into my 10 steps to financial freedom, aka your road map to prosperitytown.

This book will help you take a money load off your mind and give you the power to achieve financial independence.

Case studies

Throughout the book, we'll follow the financial fortunes of three of my clients—Sarah, Steve, and Brad and Cindy—so you can take the journey with us as I guide them through my philosophies. Their situations, goals and financial positions are all real—only their names have been changed. While their circumstances, motivations and aspirations were all vastly different when they first came to me, they now have one thing in common: using the principles discussed in this book, they were all able to realise their financial goals.

Most people would be able to relate to some aspects of the case studies. You may not have the same salary or assets, but chances are you have similar goals, investment aims, debts or financial 'personalities'. The case studies may also be representative of where you want to be. They may seem extreme, but that just proves anything is possible if you have the right tools and attitude. (Visit <www.wheresmymoney.com.au> for a complete set of financial tools for each case study. You can then use these examples as a basis for developing your own financial strategy.)

Let's meet them.

Case study 1: Sarah

Age	23
Income	$35 000
Marital status	Single
Occupation	Administration
Existing assets	Superannuation: $15 000
	Car: $7000
	Furniture: $2000
	Big-screen TV: $2000
	Cash in bank: yeah right
	Wardrobe: to die for
Existing debts	Two credit cards (total owing): $10 000
	Car loan: $10 000
	Two personal loans (total): $15 000
	Loan from grandparents: $5000
Financial 'personality'	Live for the moment; poor saver; partying with friends is her main priority. 'I'll never be able to afford a house anyway!'
	Lives beyond her means—an aspirational spender.
Sarah's story	When I first met Sarah, she was a free spirit who loved to party and have fun with her friends—just your average young person. She'd never really worried about money—there was too much other exciting stuff to do. Plus she didn't understand financial matters, so it wasn't something to dwell on.
	When her debts began to spiral out of control, she was too embarrassed to talk to anyone about it. She was devastated, scared, in a rut and couldn't see a way out. She didn't know where to start.
	Eventually, she found the courage to speak to someone. And, thankfully for her, she chose me.

Goals— personal and financial

⇨ Get this huge burden off my back and become debt-free.

⇨ Make sure I understand and manage my finances better so I never get into this position again.

⇨ Reward myself with an overseas holiday with the girls in three years' time (target: $5000). Then start saving for a house.

Strategy to achieve goals

⇨ Develop an immediate debt-reduction strategy.

⇨ Develop a savings and debt-elimination plan— increase inflows, decrease outflows, list key milestones and dates, and include rewards along the way.

⇨ Keep better track of my money in the future, and make assessing my finances a part of my weekly routine.

Case study 2: Steve

Age	35
Income	Salary: $140000
	Car allowance: $20000
	Partner's salary: $40000
Marital status	Married with two kids
Occupation	Physiotherapist
Existing assets	Property: $650000
	Superannuation: $80000
	Cars (total value): $60000 (fully financed)
	Cash in bank: $5000
	Shares: $5000
Existing debts	Home loan: $300000
	Two car loans (total): $60000
	Loan from brother-in-law: $25000
	Personal loan: $25000
	Two credit cards (total owing): $20000
	Tax debt: $15000
	Outstanding bills (e.g. rates): $4000
Financial 'personality'	Laissez-faire attitude to money. In the past Steve took money for granted—easy come, easy go. He never delved too far into his finances—it was all a little too complex and, well, boring.
Steve's story	At a young age Steve came into a significant amount of money from a promising sports career. He knew he wanted to invest some of this money for the future, so he bought a house.
	Some years later, thanks to the appreciating property market, Steve was able to leverage against his house and invest in a business. Unfortunately, he didn't appraise the business venture fully and it went under.

**Steve's story
(cont'd)**

Steve felt like the world was against him, and he couldn't see a way out of the mess. Worse still, he didn't know where to turn.

**Goals—
personal and
financial**

➪ Get myself out of this hole.

➪ Relieve the pressure that these debts are having on my marriage.

➪ Get even and start my financial journey again.

**Strategy to
achieve goals**

➪ Clear debts.

➪ Start afresh, with a better understanding and appreciation of money.

➪ Gain a greater insight into how to appraise future investment opportunities.

Case study 3: Brad and Cindy

Age	43 and 42
Income	$90 000 (combined)
Marital status	Married with two kids and one on the way
Occupation	Brad: sales representative
	Cindy: administration assistant
Existing assets	House: $500 000
	Superannuation: $120 000
	Cash in bank: $30 000
	Shares: $20 000
	Caravan: $10 000
Existing debts	Home loan: $200 000
	Credit card (total owing): $8000
Financial 'personality'	Financially naive. Looking to get out of the rat race and one day own a small business — like Brad's dad had done.
Brad and Cindy's story	When an opportunity presented itself to break free of the nine to five and get into business Brad and Cindy wanted to take it. However, neither had done anything like this before — they'd never even had an accountant. (Didn't know what they were missing, if you ask me — once you've had a numbers man, you never go back …)
	They'd spent the early part of their life travelling and enjoying the good life, but felt it was time to settle down and make something of their financial position while they were young enough.
	They admitted they didn't know the first thing about business, but they were prepared to give it a go. It was in Brad's blood, and Cindy was supportive of his dream.
	They had the goal in mind and the determination — they just needed to know how to go about achieving it.
Goals — personal and financial	▷ Get out of the rat race, control our own destiny, push ourselves and have a red-hot go at buying a small business.

Goals— personal and financial *(cont'd)*	⇨ Set ourselves up so we're not living week to week.
	⇨ Eventually buy an investment property or two and start a share portfolio. We want our money to work for us (we've heard the saying, but don't know how to actually do it).
Strategy to achieve goals	⇨ Education—particularly leverage.
	⇨ Support and reassurance with business investment decisions.

Chapter 1

Understanding money

What you'll discover in this chapter:

- what money is and why we all need it
- how to work out your net disposable income
- the common money mistakes everyone makes and how you can avoid them
- the importance of a wealthy attitude
- know where you're going—start with the end in mind.

Poets have waxed lyrical about it. Musicians have crooned over it. Rappers have, well, rapped about getting it. Cuba Gooding Jr just wanted to see it.

Money is everywhere. It's inescapable—a part of modern life. Don't feel bad for wanting a little extra of the folding stuff. You work damn hard for it—you *should* have something to show for all your effort. The good news is, you *can* have money and *still* have a life. The two aren't mutually exclusive.

Money's not only my job, it's my passion. Don't get me wrong, I'm not some Gordon Gekko freak who chases money at all costs. I simply love helping people (who don't think they can) achieve—and exceed—their financial dreams. I tell my clients that the first step to getting more money in their life is to get their head right; and to do this, you need to understand the psychology of money.

We live in an age of unparalleled prosperity, where we've 'never had it so good'. So why are so many of us struggling to make ends meet? Where does it all go? How can you make it work for you, rather than the other way around?

Before we start to uncover the answers to these questions, let's take a look at what money actually is and why we need it (I know, I know, it sounds a little obvious, but trust me, I'm an accountant). I round out this action-packed chapter by asking, 'So where's my money? Why don't I ever have enough?'

What is money and why do we need it?

The Macquarie Dictionary defines money as 'gold, silver, or other metal … issued as a medium of exchange and measure of value'; 'coin or certificate (as banknotes, etc.) generally accepted in payment of debts and current transactions'; 'wealth reckoned in terms of money'.

I prefer terms such as 'coin', 'folding', 'moolah' and any number of other euphemisms. But what does it really mean?

In layman's terms, money is a necessary evil for all of us living in modern western society. As they say, 'cash is king' (or, as a sign held aloft at the 1987 Wimbledon final said: 'Cash is better than a Czech'. But I digress.).

Money is a means to an end. We live in a world where we need money to eat, live and clothe ourselves. We've all heard someone say, 'Oh, money's not that important to me'. (Usually the people who don't have any, funnily enough.) But whether you like it or not, money is important to everyone — unless of course you live off the land a la the bush tucker man, eating witchetty grubs and the like. Or maybe your next-door neighbour has a market garden for a backyard and you procure his famous monster zucchinis in exchange for milk from the goat you've got hitched to the Hills Hoist.

For the rest of us, money is vital for our survival and wellbeing.

Needs versus wants

We need money to feed, clothe and shelter our family, to educate ourselves and our children, to have a bit of fun, and to live a life of reasonable comfort—enjoying the nicer things in life from time to time. But luxury is relative, depending on your circumstances. The first step in understanding money is to discern between *needs* and *wants*.

Needs are fundamental elements such as food, clothing, shelter, safety and physical wellbeing. To a lesser extent, needs also include things like education and training, so you can get a job (or a better one). I've argued with my fairer half till I'm blue in the face that a quiet beer with my colleagues on a Friday night is a need, but she won't buy it.

Wants are generally luxury items such as plasma TVs, home-theatre systems, overseas holidays, a new car, fancy dinners and the odd expensive bottle of wine. We could do without them if really pressed, but sometimes it's easy to overlook this, especially in today's want-it-all-and-be-quick-smart-about-it society. Most of us have been guilty of thinking, 'If only I had that new mobile phone, my life would be so much better'. Alas, as with most wants, you soon realise after a few weeks of fun that that particular want has been replaced by another one. And another after that.

The moral is cut down on *wants* that you really don't *need*, and use that money to improve your financial situation. Sounds pretty straightforward, right? We all understand this intellectually, but like most of the simple philosophies in this book, it's another step entirely to live it. My aim is to give you the tools and techniques to do just that.

In my dealings with clients—including successful businesspeople—the first thing we do is review their spending habits to categorise purchases as needs or wants. Although a simple exercise, it demonstrates the amount of spending they could do without if push really came to shove. Your level of wants, or desires, is often dependent upon your level of income.

Let's look at a real-life example. When 23-year-old Sarah came to me, she was drowning in a tsunami of debt, which included credit card debts and loans from five different lending institutions (even her grandparents). She owed a staggering $40 000.

The first thing we did was a needs versus wants analysis. When we looked at her spending, it was apparent her new furniture and big TV were excessive, as she lived with her parents—they were wants rather than needs. (An option would have been to buy second-hand.)

Given her financial state, her car was also a luxury, so I suggested she sell it and catch public transport. Also, her spending on clothes just wasn't commensurate with her situation. I encouraged Sarah to make do with what she had and not worry about keeping pace with well-dressed colleagues (you can imagine the look of horror on Sarah's face when I started dishing out wardrobe advice).

Only after you've followed Sarah's perfectly-fine-no-need-to-buy-another suit, and determined your needs and wants, are you ready to develop a financial plan (something I discuss in more detail in chapter 4).

Show me (where) the money (is)!

If you're anything like me, you've often wondered where all your money has gone by the end of each pay cycle. All our hard work and nothing to show for it. Where does all our money get to? Before unravelling that mystery, let's first look at the different ways we get cash.

Most of us generate income by getting paid for our time—that is, we work. One of the ways of getting more money is to increase how much we earn. This can be done in a number of ways such as working overtime, getting a second job, getting a better paying job, undertaking additional study and working harder to get a promotion—the common theme being hard work (and, invariably, a reduction in quality time with loved ones). (This is explored further in chapter 5.)

Another option, however, is to extricate yourself from the rat race (as advocated by Robert Kiyosaki in his amazing book *Rich Dad, Poor Dad*) by working *smarter*, not harder, using leverage. This may be putting your money into income-producing investments (property or shares, or both), or even starting or investing in a business. (These options are outlined in chapters 6 to 10. In fact, buying your first home and buying an investment property or two are such an important part of your wealth creation journey that I've dedicated three chapters to them.)

While income is fine and dandy, it's usually our level of outgoings (what we spend) that's the hidden budget-killer. That's why it's more pertinent to talk in terms of net disposable income (NDI)—income less expenses. Take Steve, for example. He was earning a hefty $140000 a year and his wife was making $40000. He even had a $20000 car allowance, bringing his total household income to $200000. Most of us would be pretty chuffed with this scenario. So how come he's got less folding than his next-door neighbour, Dan Theman?

Steve's problem is not related to income—he's got plenty. His problem is that he's outlaying too much, so his net disposable income is killing him. Take a look at table 1.1 to see how the income and expenses of Steve and Dan affect their net disposable income.

Table 1.1: comparison of net disposable income

Income per annum	Steve	Dan Theman
Wage	$140000	$70000
Car allowance	$20000	N/A
Partner's income	$40000	$60000
Total household income	$200000	$130000
Total outflows (inc. tax)	$205000	$80000
Net disposable income	**–$5000**	**$50000**

Steve ended up with a *negative* disposable income—that is, he's spending more than he earns. His outflows include his home loan, car repayments, credit card debt, household necessities (food, utilities and so on), and too many non-essentials (an outdoor setting here, a TV there ...).

To get ahead financially, the idea is to save or invest a net disposable income surplus. Steve was doing the opposite. As a consequence, Steve was living off his credit card (thus increasing his debt, when he should have been reducing it). He was also using his home loan redraw facility to withdraw cash, which increased the amount he owed the bank—precisely what the banks want you to do! And it was reducing the equity in his home.

Those of us like Steve, however, need to realise that working harder is not the only way to generate more income. Sometimes it's as easy as considering cheaper alternatives. Steve was spending big money on creche ($225 per week), when he hadn't even looked at family day care ($45 per week—a saving of $180 per week). I also suggested he cancel the gym membership of $60 per month and instead go for a run or a swim.

The more you earn, the more you spend

We've seen from Steve's example that a big income doesn't always translate to a high net disposable income. Allow me to further illustrate this fundamental point using a topic that's very dear to my heart—me.

I started my financial journey when I was 13. My first job was selling footy records at Windy Hill, home of my beloved AFL team, Essendon. Often I'd earn between $100 and $150 every second Saturday—a truckload of money for a young fella. Of course, I spent the lot—on clothes, chocolate, the odd cigarette (it was purely peer-group pressure, Mum). At the end of the fortnight, I was left with $20 or $30 in the skyrocket. So I'd go back next fortnight and earn my $150, and the cycle continued.

My next job was working at a supermarket at age 16. I was earning $250 a week doing a Thursday–Friday–Saturday shift—again, a heap of money for a youngster. Although I was bringing in more than before, my wants and needs had also increased (the more you earn …). Also, my addiction to nicotine had really kicked in (damn my influential friends, leading me astray) and I'd been welcomed into the wonderful world of alcohol with open arms. So despite my increased income, I was still left with only $20 or $30 at the end of the pay cycle. Nowhere near enough to fund my boy-about-town lifestyle.

This continued at my first grown-up job, which was a graduate accountant at Ford Motor Company. Despite now earning $35 000 a year, I'd still find myself down to $30 at the end of the fortnight. There were presents for girlfriends, petrol (at the *outrageous* price of 80 cents a litre), a TV for my bedroom, holidays and the odd social drink with friends (but only on days ending in 'y').

It wasn't until I started my own business that it dawned on me: my expenses had simply been rising in proportion to my income. I realised that before I spent money on my needs and (mostly) wants, I should be putting some away—either for investing or saving, or just for a rainy day—that was in direct proportion to what I earned. From that point on, I set aside a set percentage of my earnings; this formed the basis of my savings plan.

Savings plans—good enough for the ancient Babylonians, good enough for you!

We think we're pretty enlightened about money in modern Western society, yet we keep repeating the same fundamental mistakes of a hundred years ago—and beyond. *The Richest Man in Babylon* by George Samuel Clason (first published in 1926) uses a collection of parables set in ancient Babylon to illustrate simple and timeless financial lessons, and it's just as relevant today as it was back when the gardens were still hanging. Clason advocates putting aside 10 per cent of your earnings as part of an investment strategy. This is pretty achievable if you put your mind to it, so I upped the ante. Rather than ending up with $30 at the end of the pay cycle, I began putting away 20 per cent of my income into my investments. And because it was being paid directly into another account, I didn't ever get to see it—or miss it. It doesn't take long to see the difference this can make. Using our case studies, table 1.2 compares the effect of different savings percentages over a year.

Table 1.2: comparison of savings percentages over one year

| Name | Income | Percentage of savings | | |
		1%	10%	20%
Sarah	$35000	$350	$3500	$7000
Steve	$200000	$2000	$20000	$40000
Brad and Cindy	$90000	$900	$9000	$18000

Combine this 10 or 20 per cent (as much as you can afford, really) with the 9 per cent compulsory superannuation contribution that your employer puts aside for you out of the kindness of their legal obligation, and things already look rosier. Which brings me, dear reader, to compound interest. Let's check out our lab rats (er, case studies) after they've put 10 per cent of their income into a basic savings account, generating 7 per cent interest, for 10 years. Table 1.3 shows the result (with their incomes adjusted for CPI).

Table 1.3: impact of compound interest on savings over time

Name	Income	Annual contribution (10% of salary)	Contributions after 10 years	Contributions after 10 years, compounding at 7% p.a. interest
Sarah	$35 000	$3 500	$35 000	$50 051
Steve	$200 000	$20 000	$200 000	$286 058
Brad and Cindy	$90 000	$9 000	$90 000	$128 700

What a sweet combination a forced savings plan and compounding interest make! Remember, their money was only invested in a regular high-interest savings account. Imagine the impact if it was invested in a more aggressive portfolio with stronger returns! In chapter 4, I'll walk you through creating your own budget and savings plan.

The importance of a 'wealthy' attitude

A good friend and early mentor of mine once told me: 'Jeremy,'—he was a genius with money, but terrible with names—'if you want to be rich, *act* rich'. There's no doubt in my mind that visual perception really works. I used the same technique in my youthful glory days playing Aussie Rules football. In the warm-up I'd visualise taking spectacular marks, kicking booming goals, picking the ball up with a graceful flourish, crashing recklessly into opponents. When I was in that positive frame of mind before a game, I was unstoppable on the field.

I still use visualisation. If I'm preparing for a client meeting or a speaking engagement, I'll close my eyes and imagine taking an incredible mark … 20 highlight-filled minutes later, I'll start thinking about performing well in the actual meeting. Only once have I tackled a client by mistake. He was a lot smaller than me so thankfully I wasn't harmed.

Perception versus reality

Adopting a positive attitude is vital—not just in business, sport or personal finance, but in all aspects of life. The way you portray and conduct yourself can influence the people and situations you encounter. You could say that, in some areas, you attract much of what happens to you in life.

When my business partner and I first started The Practice we earned a wage of only $2500 each in our first year. But we always looked and acted like we were successful. We tapped into our savings to buy expensive suits, freshly pressed shirts, beautiful ties, immaculate shoes, frilly knickers (did I just type that...?). We acted like we were already rich and never once lamented our perilous financial situation.

As part of this positive visualisation, it's important to focus on what you want, not what you don't. If you focus on the negative, that's usually what you end up with. Rather than saying, 'I'm sick of being overweight and unfit', it's better to say, 'I'm looking forward to getting a six-pack (and not one I've just taken out of the fridge)'.

Some of my younger clients have already amassed significant debts. As mentioned earlier, Sarah had racked up $40000 in debt by the time she came to me. But the important thing was she faced up to her problems. It can seem easier to bury your head in the sand and ignore them, but that will only make them worse. The only way to fix a problem is to face up to it.

Rather than dwell on her debts, I helped Sarah focus on the end outcome: the day she was debt-free and could sleep safe in the knowledge that the debt collector wouldn't call around the next morning. We then put some debt-reduction strategies in place and reduced her spending (I'll outline her saving plan in chapter 4). She took on weekend work to increase her earnings, sold some assets on eBay and, over the course of two years, that $40000 debt was steadily whittled away.

Focusing on the outcome you want will help you to achieve your desired goal a lot faster. When you dwell on the negatives, all you see is obstacles blocking your path. By focusing on what you want, those obstacles become challenges—and you can find ways to overcome them.

Know where you're going—the importance of setting goals

To achieve any objective, you first need to know what it is. We all want financial prosperity, but what does that mean to you? Most people are too busy living life (or avoiding it) to set long-term financial goals. Others don't want to overemphasise the importance of money (yet still lament that they never have enough). We tend to focus on the next big purchase, rather than looking at the big financial picture. However, to get ahead it's essential to set goals and have a clear vision of where you are—and where you want to be. You need to plan to achieve this goal and regularly visualise attaining it. (Goal setting and having a vision are discussed further in chapter 4.)

Start with the end in mind

'Start with the end in mind' is a phrase you often hear in business. To run a successful enterprise, one of the first things you should do is focus on the end (not the rapture ... the day you sell your business). Say to yourself, 'I'm looking at this business with the aim of selling it one day. How should I run it, what should we do and what should it look like so that a prospective purchaser will pay me a lot of money for it?'

I often encourage business owners to remove themselves from the business, as they are typically the biggest limiting factor to its success. The emotional attachment, psychological baggage and ego can all sabotage even the best-laid business plans. (The specific needs of business owners are looked at more closely in chapter 10.)

The same philosophy holds true with our personal wealth-creation goals and dreams. If you don't have a target to aim for, you'll never get there. You need to identify what you're trying to achieve. Every individual's circumstances and desired outcomes are different: some people want to live comfortably in retirement; some focus on being debt-free; others want to get out of the rat race, stop working for an employer and start their own business. So it's vital to determine what outcomes we need to achieve these goals. Usually it's an amount of money or a value of income-producing assets, whether that be $800, $50 000 or $2 million — but we need to identify what that is so we can develop a strategy to get us there.

Never give up!

Persistence is perhaps the most important concept I want to convey to you. It doesn't matter how dire your situation is: keep plugging away and things have a habit of working out in the end.

I'm not suggesting you just keep doing the same old thing. Benjamin Franklin famously said the definition of insanity is to do the same thing over and over, expecting a different result. You have to be smart and implement a carefully considered plan, but once that's in place, stick to it.

Remember our friend Sarah? Well, not long after coming to me out of her mind with worry over her $40 000 debt, her car broke down. Another $3000. Then she fell ill and needed an operation (no, this is not an episode of *Neighbours*) — and, of course, having little net disposable income, she'd let her health insurance lapse. Another $4000. At this point, her debts had reached $47 LARGE. But rather than throw her hands in the air, cry 'Why me?' and hit the bottle (I thought about suggesting it), she stuck to her savings plan and got busy with extra weekend work, and I'm thrilled to say that at the time of publishing she was debt-free. You go girl!

I love the quote from Thomas Edison, inventor and entrepreneur: 'I have not failed. I've just found 10 000 ways that won't work'. Where would we be if he'd given up on his experiments with electric light after the first few attempts? (With an enormous matches bill, that's where.)

This was brought home to me—literally—when my dad lost his business (and everything else) at the age of 30. Rather than feel sorry for himself, he and Mum soldiered on, with Dad working four jobs, until the hard work and extreme dedication finally paid off, and he once again became a success.

A common theme to every success story is losing it all along the way, but remaining focused on the light at the end of the tunnel, and having the determination to persevere when the going gets tough. Some see failure as a reaffirmation of their negative self-opinion; successful people see failure as a lesson—an experience to learn from.

You deserve financial success

Before we really get stuck into your new financial journey, I want to tell you something: you *deserve* to be financially secure. Prosperous, even. Many people I meet just don't see eye to eye with money. They view it warily, suspiciously. For them, it's not a door to a more comfortable life—it's a mysterious, vaguely scary entity. Mostly, they feel they don't deserve it—sometimes because their parents have struggled and they feel that's their birthright. Well, you need to break free of this limiting belief and realise that we all deserve prosperity. And we can all achieve it.

Financial success is no different to success in any other sphere of human endeavour, be it sport, politics or relationships. If you don't believe you deserve something or don't think you'll attain it, you'll be proven right.

This book is all about demystifying money—showing you the many ways you can get it and keep it. The first step is developing the goal to become more financially secure, and being prepared to roll up your sleeves to make it happen. So get yourself a wealthy mindset and let's get busy making you some serious coin!

Jay's take aways

- Money is an important, inescapable part of modern life.

- Review your spending habits to identify the percentage spent on wants (or luxuries) and the percentage spent on needs (those mandatory necessities).

- When analysing your financial situation, look at your net disposable income—income less expenses.

- To improve your financial position you can either increase your income or decrease your spending (but beware: the 'more you earn, more you spend').

- For many of us, the main option to generate additional income is to increase our salary—by working harder or longer, studying to improve our value or getting a new job.

- Financially savvy people work *smarter*, not harder, using leverage. Invest in an income-producing asset such as shares, property or a business.

- The best way to save is to transfer a percentage of your income into a savings account at the time you receive it (ideally, up to 20 per cent of your income).

- Compound interest multiplies your savings efforts.

- It's vital to have a wealthy attitude. You attract much of what happens to you in your life, so act in a wealthy manner (without spending all your money), visualise where you want to be and don't dwell on the negatives.

- You need a clear goal of where you want to get to on your financial journey. Focus on what you want and start with the end in mind.

- Don't give up when things get tough. Face up to your problems and look at every failure as a learning experience.

- You deserve to be financially successful—but, as they say with money, you have to earn it.

Chapter 2

Understanding your financial personality

What you'll discover in this chapter:

ŏ what your financial personality is

ŏ how to establish your income and expenses

ŏ how to use tools such as budget planners and asset and liability statements to clearly define your current situation

ŏ types of investment risk, and how to determine your risk profile

ŏ the importance of safeguarding against unforeseen circumstances.

In most facets of life, we're all different—be it our ideals, beliefs, music tastes or footy team. Our differing viewpoints and personalities apply equally when it comes to money—you could say we all have a 'financial personality'. Understanding yours is the first step to taking control of your finances.

What's your financial personality?

How would you describe your financial personality? Some people are spendthrift—as soon as they get it, they just can't help getting rid of it (you'd get on well with my wife). Others wouldn't open their wallet even at gunpoint (just ask my business partner, Rob—we've been in business for 11 years and I'm *still* waiting for him to shout me lunch).

Then there are the religious savers who are disciplined enough to not only create a budget, but also to stick to it.

And of course there are the people who, no matter how hard they work or how much they earn, just never seem to have any cash in the bank. They're not necessarily irresponsible with their money, they just cruise along and don't really think about their spending habits, let alone develop any sort of financial plan. They may do okay financially, so weekly saving is not a huge focus, but, gee, it'd be nice to hang onto a little more of it and have something more to show for all the hard work.

To work out what your financial personality (or 'sign') is, take a look at table 2.1. Chances are you'll be a combination of two or more personalities.

Table 2.1: so ... what sign are you?

Financial star sign	Typical traits
Ostrich	Don't want to know anything about money. I'll never have any and if I had it, I'd probably lose it. Better to bury my head in the sand and not even think about it.
Chicken	The average Joe or Joanne. Responsible and risk-averse. Does the bare minimum: goes to work, gets paid, pays off credit card or mortgage, but that's it. Will never get ahead.
Kookaburra	Too busy partying and having fun to be bothered with financial stuff. Couldn't care less about saving—tomorrow is *so* far away!
Peacock	Loves splashing the cash! And wants as many people as possible to see. Reckless with money—even though they may earn a lot, it's usually not spent in income-producing ways.
Eagle	Plans ahead. Takes a considered, long-term view. Sees the big picture—a little pain now can be very, very beneficial in the long run.
Magpie	Mad saver. In fact, hates opening the wallet for anything.

We can see these personalities in action by looking at the case studies. Sarah was a 'kookaburra'. She was having a ball, but it all caught up with her. Big time. Steve was a 'peacock'—he loved to spend and outdo the next person. Brad and Cindy were 'chickens' when they came to me. But they knew it—and that knowledge gave them the ability to change their situation, and their life, forever. I'd consider myself an 'eagle'. I'm not blowing my own trumpet, it's just a fact. Hey, you wouldn't have bought this book if I was anything else, right?

Even though we're all different there are some universal truths we all must face if we're to master our money, regardless of our financial situation:

- We need to make more than we spend—that is, have a surplus.
- With that surplus we need to:
  - squirrel some of it away in case of unforeseen emergencies
  - invest some additional cash to generate real wealth, so it can 'work' for us and provide additional income.
- We need to protect our money so it can't be taken away from us (whether by a person or an event).

Where the bloody hell am I? Identifying your income and expenses

The first step to breaking the shackles and achieving financial independence is working out where you're at now—that is, understanding what you've got to work with to help you generate wealth. As with all effective plans, this needs to be fully articulated and the best way to do this is to write it down.

First, identify all your sources of income. For most people, their salary is their main source. Other types of income may include:

- rent from investment properties
- dividends from shares
- distributions from managed investments
- interest from bank or high-interest savings accounts
- income from a business.

Second, list your expenses. To do this properly, I recommend you take the time to examine your expenditure in a typical week (or, if possible, a month or even a quarter). Go through your credit card and bank statements to ensure you capture every item you spend money on, no matter how incidental. Believe you me, I know the process is cumbersome, time-consuming and sometimes painful — I do this every time a statement arrives — but it becomes a powerful tool, particularly if your financial personality means you usually spend more than you should. It can be confronting to know what percentage of your income is spent on wants rather than needs, but it's an important part of controlling your expenditure.

It doesn't take as long as you think and provides many benefits, including:

- ensuring your statements are accurate (particularly important for credit card transactions) and alerting you to any questionable transactions

- highlighting where — and exactly how much — you spend

- allowing you to compare your actual expenditure to your budget so you can track your performance.

Having established your income and expenses, and drawn up a budget, the next step is to list your assets and liabilities. From here, you can determine the focus of your wealth creation strategy — to increase your assets and/or reduce your liabilities. (This process is explained in more detail in chapter 4.)

Jay's hot tip

Tracking your monthly expenditure is easier if, like me, you use your credit card for most transactions. It's then just a simple process of reviewing your statement once a month.

Risk versus reward

The only way to get anywhere in life is to take risks. If you think that boy or girl is cute, you've gotta risk a broken heart (or a drink in the face) to ask them out. There's risk involved in travelling by plane, driving a car or crossing the road. So, in some ways, risk is inescapable (unless you live in a cave, and even then, you've got bear risk).

In finance, we have what's called investment risk. Any investment decision you make has an associated risk. Your decision will relate to the amount of money you are able to invest, your circumstances at the time and your needs for the future. As shown in table 2.2, the rate of return on an investment is commensurate with the level of risk. The golden rule is *the higher the expected returns, the higher the likely risk*. Understanding risk and protecting yourself is the second step on your wealth creation journey.

Table 2.2: levels of risk and return for a range of investment options

Investment option	Risk level	Average return per annum, 1998–2007 (%)
Under the mattress	Zero (except inflation!)	0
Cash	Low	6
Property	Medium	10
Australian shares	High	13

Usually when you make an informed decision to take on a certain risk, you create the opportunity for greater returns. At the same time, the potential loss may also be higher. This is called the risk–reward trade-off.

Your investment aim should be to minimise your risk, getting the right balance between the rate of return and the safety of your money. Risk is inevitable, but it can be reduced through the use of a risk-management strategy.

Generally, financial planners prepare tailored advice based on an assessment of your risk tolerance. For most investors, risk can be defined as the potential to suffer a loss of capital during the term of an investment. A more extended measure of risk may be the possibility that an investment portfolio will not achieve the required return over the investment time horizon.

There are four major asset classes in which to invest: cash, fixed interest, shares (Australian and international) and property. A financial planner will use your risk profile to determine your ideal asset allocation—that is, the blend of asset classes that best suit your circumstances, time frame and objectives.

Types of investment risk

When planning to invest, it's important to be aware of the types of risk associated with investing. There are four main types:

- *permanent loss of capital*. This is the risk the majority of investors fear the most—losing their money. The key to managing this risk is to buy quality investments and to diversify across various investments (so if one investment falls, it doesn't have a big impact on the total portfolio).

- *fluctuating returns*. You can reduce this risk by investing for the long term and not chasing last year's return. Investing is all about time *in* the market, not *timing* the market. Diversifying your assets across various asset classes can also smooth out the return.

- *not achieving your investment goals*. This typically occurs when people play it safe and invest in defensive assets (cash and fixed-interest investments)—often when markets have been performing poorly. This can result in returns that don't allow people to achieve their goals.

- *inflation*. This is the risk of doing nothing—leaving your money under the mattress, as they say. It's the risk that the purchasing power of your investment (or lack thereof) may not keep pace with inflation (inflation being the increase in the general price of goods and services). Therefore, inflation risk occurs when your investment provides a net return less than the inflation rate. Even if an investment earns money, if it's not ahead of inflation—you're losing out!

Bearing these investment risks in mind, and other factors such as your time frame and financial goals, you can determine your investor risk profile. Table 2.3 describes the various types of risk profiles. (Always get professional help to know for sure.) To give you an indication of my risk profile, I'm classed as assertive/aggressive.

Table 2.3: risk profiles

Risk profile	Investment horizon	Major asset classes
Cautious	Three years	Fixed-income securities
Cautious/prudent	Three years	Cash and fixed interest
Prudent	Four years plus	Interest-bearing securities and growth-orientated investments
Prudent/assertive	Four to five years	Growth-orientated investments
Assertive	Five to six years	Blue-chip equities and income-producing property
Assertive/aggressive	Five years plus	Shares and property
Aggressive	Seven years plus	Property and actively managed Australian and international shares

Key determinants of your risk profile

Your risk profile is determined by three main factors:

- *how long you have in the market.* There's a big difference between the risk profile of a 65 year old and a 25 year old. A younger person has the benefit of time — that is, time in the market. They can therefore ride out fluctuations. Investments go up and down, but over time the trend is generally always up. Older investors don't have the luxury of waiting around for an investment to come good again, so they have to play it safer.

- *how you feel about fluctuations; how they would affect you.* Your risk tolerance is shaped by how much you can afford to lose. Brad and Cindy can afford to lose more than Sarah — not a lot more, but they have more income and assets, and less non-income-producing debt. Your risk tolerance is also affected by your personality. Some people hate losing money, while others have a much more 'easy come, easy go' attitude. They're prepared to risk it to make it.

- *your financial objectives.* All things being equal, everyone would love to make heaps of cash quickly. Unfortunately, some of us don't have the ready cash to invest or we've got debts to pay off first. So you need to base your investment risk around your situation and your objectives.

Let's take a look at some examples using our case studies.

Being 23, you'd assume Sarah would be an aggressive investor—she's got plenty of time to ride out fluctuations. However, other factors come into play. Her goal is debt reduction, meaning she needs to put all available revenue into paying off her loans. She can't afford any downward fluctuations. Therefore, she's a 'cautious' investor.

Steve's already got a significant asset—his home; however, like a lot of Australians, his asset allocation is overweighted in property. There are no major asset purchases on the short-term horizon, so he doesn't need to access his cash within five years. Thus, he can afford to be more aggressive in his investment strategy, putting him in the 'assertive/aggressive' category.

Brad and Cindy not only want to start a business, they want an investment property within three years. They're focused on saving $60 000 for a deposit. Any spare cash they can put away needs to be accessible in three years. So even though they're well set up financially, they still can't afford to wear fluctuations. This makes them reasonably cautious investors, falling into the 'prudent' category.

'At least I've got my health'—the importance of risk management

It may seem like a cliché, but our health really is the most important asset we have. Without it we can't generate an income, and it's hard to enjoy the fruits of our labour (which is half the reason for our labour in the first place). Most people never think anything bad will ever happen to them (just as well, otherwise we'd probably never leave the house). But I urge you to stop and consider the impact on you and your family should something unforeseen happen that affects your ability to generate income or your wellbeing.

Take a moment to think about the following questions:

- If you couldn't earn an income, what would happen to your lifestyle? Could you still maintain your financial commitments (such as home loan repayments or car lease)?

- What if your health was affected by a stroke or heart attack? Could you afford the time off work, not to mention the hospital bills?

- What if you or your partner were to pass away? Could the family still get by financially without you?

Risk management is the process of protecting you and your family from any unforeseen events affecting your ability to generate income and/or additional expenses you may incur.

Insuring your most important asset — you

Most people are turned off insurance due to its perceived cost and the fact you have nothing to show for your outlay. While it may be an additional expense, consider the costs of *not* being covered. Personally, the thought of my family being left to fend for themselves overcomes my reluctance to fork out for insurance. I'm insured to the eyeballs: life, income, you name it. In fact, to my family, financially I'm better off dead!

We all accept the need to insure our cars, which on average are worth only $25 000. Yet, for a similar amount, we can insure our most important asset — ourselves, and our ability to earn income (I'm sure you value yourself at more than $25 000). As long as they're structured correctly, income protection and life insurance can be tax-deductible, making them even more attractive. I see insurance as one of those necessary evils — the only thing worse than paying for it is having to claim on it.

Jay's hot tip

Check out <www.wheresmymoney.com.au> to discover how affordable personal insurance really is. The insurance calculator will give you a guide to your available options.

Risk insurances

Bad things happen — not that they'll happen to *you*, of course... it's always to other people. No one ever expects to die or be injured; but

I urge anyone with dependents or financial obligations to review the risk insurances available to you, including:

- health insurance

- life insurance

- total and permanent disablement (TPD) insurance

- income protection (and salary continuance) insurance

- trauma insurance.

Health insurance is something most people are familiar with, but let's look at the other risk insurances in detail.

Life insurance

According to the Australian Institute of Health and Welfare, in Australia, premature death is a real risk. In 2006, about 22 per cent of male deaths and 14 per cent of female deaths were of those aged between 25 and 64.

In the event of your death, life insurance (named by a true glass-half-full person) provides a lump sum to the person you nominate, called the beneficiary. It gives financial protection to your dependants, such as your spouse and kids, so they can clear debts, such as the mortgage, and provides money for them to live on. You can rest (in peace) easy, knowing the people that matter most to you are protected should you fall off the perch.

Total and permanent disablement insurance

A 1998 survey by the Australian Bureau of Statistics (ABS) reported that 3.6 million people had one or more impairments that restricted everyday activities. Of those, 2.1 million were aged between 16 and 64.

The proceeds from total and permanent disablement (TPD) insurance can be used to eliminate debt, pay ongoing medical expenses, make home modifications or hire care services such as nursing, cleaning and cooking. Again, the real benefit is peace of mind for your loved ones.

Income protection insurance

In 2007 the ABS reported that of the 10.8 million Australians who worked at some time in the 12 months to June 2006, 6.4 per cent

(690 000 people) experienced a work-related injury, with men experiencing a higher work-related injury rate than women.

Income protection insurance covers you for loss of income through illness or injury and premiums may be tax-deductible against your income. Payments equal up to 75 per cent of pre-illness or injury income while you are unable to work. This protection is vital because should illness or injury occur your regular expenses and payments will continue, as well as additional expenses that may be incurred as a result of the illness or injury. Furthermore, where one spouse is the main income generator for the household, it is imperative that his or her income is insured.

Trauma insurance

According to the Heart Foundation, more than 3.5 million Australians are affected by cardiovascular disease and about 1.4 million are disabled long term by cardiovascular disease. Gee, aren't I full of cheery little tidbits?

If those people had trauma insurance, they'd receive a lump sum payment upon diagnosis of their condition. Trauma insurance covers specified medical conditions such as cancer, stroke, heart attack, loss of limb(s) or sight or hearing, coronary disease, major head trauma and coronary artery bypass surgery. The payout helps to fund medical costs and day-to-day expenses, and can be used to clear debts so you can focus on making a full recovery.

Facing your fears

Now that we've gone through the various ways you can protect yourself against risk, I'd like you to take a few moments to write down your financial fears—those thoughts, beliefs or attitudes that stop you from achieving great things with money (and in life in general). Common examples of fear include:

- fear of failure ('I could lose everything'; 'I'll probably choose a dud investment')
- fear of the unknown ('I'm out of my depth'; 'I don't know where to start')

- once bitten, twice shy ('I had a previous investment that went belly up')

- fear of success ('I don't deserve to be wealthy'; 'I'll get taxed heaps'; 'I'll spend a fortune on advisers to hang on to it')

- distrust of financial advisers, the government and so on ('I'll get ripped off or dudded, or they'll change the rules').

Once you've created your list, I want you to focus on turning those negatives into positives. Table 2.4 provides examples of how you can do this. With the power of positive thinking, your fears can become challenges, and the challenges suddenly become opportunities—signposts towards your new life.

Table 2.4: turning your fears into opportunities

Fear	Opportunity
The stock market is too volatile—I could lose everything. Remember the 1987 crash and the dotcom bubble of 2000?	The '87 crash was over 20 years ago. Move on! If you take a long-term view (as you should with all major investments), the stock market is still a great option. To be extra safe, you can invest in capital-protected stocks that provide a guaranteed return on your investment. And, in actual fact, if you'd gone on a buying spree after the '87 crash, you would have picked up some bargains due to the sudden drop in values.
A friend made a business investment that went sour—it's too risky.	Nothing ventured, nothing gained. Perhaps your friend didn't do his or her homework properly, much like Steve. You won't lose your money if you deposit it with a big bank, but you won't make any money either. Obviously, all investments need to be fully researched (with the help of an independent expert if possible). Remember, most successful people have faced financial ruin at one time or another, but have come out stronger and wiser for the experience.
My parents had a rental property that was trashed by the tenants, costing them thousands.	There are safeguards you can take to cover yourself. Interview property managers, provide criteria for tenants and take out landlord insurance. There are also property groups that provide a guaranteed rental yield (up to five years), and a repair- and maintenance-free period.

Fear	Opportunity
I'd never increase my superannuation contributions—I can't access it until I retire and the government keeps changing the rules.	Most recent changes to superannuation have been in the consumer's favour to encourage people to invest more in their own retirement. The tax rate has been slashed to *one-third* of the individual tax rate. When you consider the tax breaks, it really becomes an attractive investment. And the fact you can't access it should be seen as a positive—you know it will continue working for you until you really need it (when you retire). (We'll look at superannuation closely in chapter 12.)
I don't earn enough money to invest.	There are investment strategies to suit everyone. Even those earning less than $30 000 per annum can start investing with only $1000 and generate a 150 per cent return!
I've seen too many dodgy financial advisers on current affairs shows to ever trust them with my money	Go and talk to several advisers until you find someone you feel comfortable with. Ask friends and colleagues for recommendations. Check out industry association websites such as CPA Australia, <www.cpaaustralia.com.au>, and the Financial Planning Association of Australia, <www.fpa.asn.au>. The Australian Securities & Investments Commission (ASIC) provides a significant level of protection to consumers of financial services, particularly with the introduction of the Australian Financial Services Reform Act and the requirement of advisers to either hold or be authorised representatives of someone with an Australian financial services licence. The best tool of all is arming yourself with a basic financial understanding, so you are fully aware of the particular strategy the adviser recommends. Ask him or her to provide regular performance updates so you know how you're tracking.
With all my monthly expenses, I don't have any residual to invest—I barely seem to have enough money to get by week to week.	You're looking at it the wrong way—first, work out how much you should be saving. Take the opportunity to review your monthly spending and find ways to create savings. You can also invest 10 to 20 per cent of your earnings *before* you start spending (via automatic transfer from your pay), to ensure you stick to your savings plan.

Table 2.4 *(cont'd)*: turning your fears into opportunities

Fear	Opportunity
I've never been good with finance stuff—I'd probably make the wrong investment.	By empowering yourself with finance knowledge, finding trusted advisers and spreading your risk, you greatly improve your likelihood of success.
I don't deserve to be wealthy; my family are good, honest Aussie battlers.	This is your chance to take control and make yourself wealthy, so your children don't start their journey thinking like that. There's no such thing as 'deservedness' when it comes to money. Some of Australia's richest people, such as Richard Pratt and Lindsay Fox, came from humble beginnings.
Being wealthy scares me—what if I lose it all? Better not to have it in the first place; life will be simpler and less complicated.	Yes, being wealthy comes with added responsibility such as paying more attention to your financial situation. And there's bound to be added stress from time to time—what if you want a new car, but your wife wants an overseas holiday?
I don't know where to start.	You've already started the education process by reading this book. The more you educate yourself about your finances, the more you can take control of your future.

Jay's take aways

- Know yourself. Discovering your 'financial personality' and the impact it's having on your wealth creation opportunities is the first step to taking control of your finances.

- Universal money truths: make more than you spend; save a surplus; invest additional cash; and protect your money or assets.

- Understand your current financial position—take the time to examine your income, expenses, assets and liabilities so you know what you're working with.

- Review your credit card and bank statements each month to understand and monitor your expenditure.

- The rate of return on an investment is commensurate with the level of risk—the higher the expected returns, the higher the likely risk.

- Types of investment risk include permanent loss of capital, fluctuating returns, not achieving your investment goals and inflation risk (the risk of doing nothing).

- Your aversion to investment risks, and other factors, such as your time frame and financial goals, will determine your investor risk profile—anywhere from cautious to aggressive.

- Your most important asset is *you*. Protect yourself from unforeseen events that may affect your ability to generate income and/or additional expenses you may incur.

- Your fears stop you from achieving great things with money (and life).

- Every successful person has lost the lot at least once—it all depends on how you react to life's challenges. Successful people look at failure as a learning experience, and become stronger and wiser because of it.

Chapter 3

The 'c' word

> **What you'll discover in this chapter:**
> ♦ credit: the good, the bad and the interest free
> ♦ the pros and cons of drawing on your equity
> ♦ the ins and outs of the various finance options available today
> ♦ the concept of delayed gratification
> ♦ credit card traps and how to avoid them.

The big concern I have about our modern-day money mindset is our attitude to credit. It's never been easier to get money. Buying a house on credit is one thing, as we are (usually) purchasing an asset that will appreciate in value. But our credit reliance extends to smaller purchases. We can easily buy furniture, whitegoods, electrical items—whatever we want—on up to 48 months interest free (and in my experience, anything that sounds too good to be true, usually is). Take, for example, our case study subject, Sarah, and the problems easy money caused her.

This credit availability is most pronounced in the way we buy property. Just 25 years ago, people would save for a 50 per cent deposit. These days it's not uncommon for people to borrow up to—and sometimes over—100 per cent of the property price. This is okay if prices continue to rise and interest rates remain steady, but if recent times have shown us anything when investing, it's to expect the unexpected.

Easy money is not the culprit here—it's what we do with it that gets us in trouble. So rather than say there's 'good' and 'bad' credit, I'd say there are good and bad *uses* of credit, some of which are outlined in table 3.1. Bear in mind, I'm not saying you can't buy these things; of course you need to reward yourself occasionally. Just don't use credit to pay for them—save until you can afford them! Consolidating bad debt is the third step to getting more money in your life.

Table 3.1: 'good' and 'bad' uses of credit

Bad uses of credit	Good uses of credit
Buying furniture	Investing in shares
Buying luxury items (e.g. boats)	Buying an investment property
Going on a holiday	Investing in a business
Extending your dwelling	

Personal finance options

There are a lot more personal finance options available today than there were 20 years ago. It's hard to believe, but back then there were no credit cards, no 24-month interest-free periods, no easy personal loans and it was a lot harder to get a home loan. So it's easier for young people like Sarah to get into deep financial trouble than it was for Brad and Cindy at the same age.

Today's personal finance options include:

- short-term finance
- personal loans
- pawn shops
- loan sharks

- bad credit experts
- mum and dad.

All these options have pros and cons. However, I urge you to use loan sharks and bad credit experts as an absolute last resort. Some can cause you more pain and suffering due to their enormous loan establishment costs and interest rates. Also, there are extreme consequences if you don't pay out the loan. Likewise, owing money to family and/or friends can carry with it another problem—guilt. Sometimes, that can be worse!

Jay's hot tip

Unless purchasing an appreciating, income-generating asset—if you don't have the money, don't buy it!

It's interesting to compare today's attitude to credit with the attitude during the 1970s, when I was a kid. Instead of all the credit options available today, we had lay-by. If you wanted something but didn't have the cash, you put it on lay-by and paid it off over a certain period of time. Only then could you take the prized possession home with you. The beauty of this was you had an incentive to pay the item off as quickly as possible.

That mentality has changed. Today, there's no inducement to pay off your credit debt (apart from interest penalties if you don't pay the minimum amount). In our 'want it now' society, we have to have everything that our friends and neighbours have *right now*—and (sometimes to our detriment) we can get it now. Plenty of retailers now offer up to 48 months interest free through a range of different finance companies. Your only requirement is to make the minimum repayment every month. This can be great in the short term, but if you read the fine print, those minimum recommended repayments don't include much of the principal, so at the end of the term you're left still owing a significant chunk of the purchase price—at an astronomical interest rate.

This was a big part of Sarah's problem. When furnishing her bedroom, she didn't read the fine print, and at the end of her interest-free period she was left with a mountain of debt (at excruciatingly high interest rates). So take the time to crunch the numbers and ensure you pay enough each month to avoid being left with a bouncing baby debt at the end of the term.

Car finance

The way we buy cars has also evolved. The percentage of cars purchased via a lending option these days versus those purchased outright has skyrocketed. For my clients in business or with the ability to claim a percentage of the interest associated with a vehicle purchase as a tax deduction (that is, those that use their car for work-related purposes), financing the purchase as opposed to using your savings makes sense. They are much better off using their cash to pay down non-deductible debt, such as a loan on your dwelling, or investing in an income-generating, appreciating asset such as shares or an investment property.

The typical lending options available for car finance are as follows:

- lease payments
- hire purchase
- chattel mortgage
- personal loan.

The first three have very similar characteristics (in the eyes of the consumer)—an interest rate, a monthly repayment amount and a residual component. However, their treatment, particularly for tax purposes, is vastly different, so be careful and seek professional advice about which style of finance will suit your circumstances. Also watch the size of the residual (anywhere from 0 per cent to 50 per cent) and the term of the loan (usually three to five years).

Table 3.2 outlines the tax treatment of the various car finance options available.

Table 3.2: tax treatment of car finance options

Lending option	Tax treatment
Lease payments	The total payment is tax-deductible (you're effectively renting the asset).
Hire purchase and chattel mortgage	The interest component is deductible, not the principal payments. However, with higher purchase and chattel mortgage you take ownership of the vehicle immediately; therefore, you can claim depreciation (loss of value) as an expense.
Personal loan	Similar to hire purchase and chattel mortgages, you take ownership of the car and can therefore claim depreciation and interest costs as a tax deduction.

Residual amount

A common practice when financing a vehicle is to only finance a percentage of the vehicle and leave what's called a residual amount. This is the amount outstanding at the end of the finance term. Once you pay it, you own the asset outright. The size of the residual depends on the amount of your monthly repayments—the higher your monthly payments, the more you pay towards the asset during the term and the lower the residual at the end of the lease.

At the end of the lease term, you need to pay the residual—either out of your own pocket or by selling the car (trading the car in to the dealership or through a private sale). Make sure you do your own homework. Car dealers will often encourage you to take a finance option that has a higher residual at the end of the term, as this option gives you lower monthly repayments, meaning the car is more affordable in the short term (thus increasing the likelihood that you'll buy the car). This is great for them, but not necessarily great for you. The downside is you may be left with a shortfall at the end of the period. Your car may not be worth the residual owing on it.

To be on the safe side, as a minimum, go with a three-year arrangement with a 40 per cent residual and change cars at the end of the term. To give yourself more breathing space at the end of the contract you can set the residual at 30 per cent.

Accessing equity—drawing the curtain on drawdowns

Over the last few years, the value of property has increased significantly, making many ordinary folk 'rich' on paper. The massive appreciation of their (non-income-producing) asset has given many people access to equity (and, seemingly, a licence to spend it). We're able to draw down (withdraw funds) on an asset (such as our home) to buy:

- luxuries such as furniture, a big-screen TV or holiday
- income-producing assets such as property or shares, or invest in a business.

This is clearly illustrated in table 3.3 where case studies 2 and 3 are compared.

Table 3.3: comparison of drawdown techniques

	Case study 2: Steve	Case study 3: Brad and Cindy
Type of purchase	Luxury items (e.g. spa, furniture, kitchen renovation, holiday)	Deposit for an investment property (with a purchase price of $400 000)
Amount drawn down	$80 000	$80 000, and an interest-only loan for the balance of $320 000
Appreciation or depreciation of the purchase over 10 years	Dramatic depreciation	If you buy the right property in the right area, chances are it will double in value over 10 years. It's safe to assume that Brad and Cindy's property will be worth $800 000, while their loan stays at $320 000. Therefore, their equity has grown from $80 000 to $480 000!

Jay's hot tip

You *can* use the equity in your home—just try to use it for good instead of evil (those 'good' and 'bad' assets mentioned earlier in the chapter).

Plastic fantastic

Credit cards are great. Hardly anyone could do without them in today's world. Who doesn't love having a big wad of someone else's money at our fingertips anytime we 'need' to buy something! But it gets better—banks reward us for using our cards by giving us points towards free stuff. It's almost too good to be true, right? Right. As handy as they are, there's a downside to credit cards that everyone needs to understand.

The way most of us use credit cards is a big concern for me. I should know—I see the effects time and time again among clients who wind up mired in out-of-control debt. The problems start when we begin our credit card courtship with the banks. Like any relationship, things start off great—they woo us and tell us how much they love us, and any time we pay off a portion of our debt, they tell us how fabulous we are and ask if we'd like even *more* money that isn't ours to play with. It's pretty hard to resist, especially when we've come to rely on using other people's money to fund our lifestyle. We are then showered in gifts (reward points) to entice us to buy more stuff on credit.

However, miss one anniversary (or, in this case, a monthly payment) and the honeymoon is over. The banks turn, treating us like a jilted lover: scratching our CDs and throwing our possessions out on the street (well, they charge us interest at around 20 per cent, but you get my drift).

Easy money

Getting a credit card is so easy these days. Professionals (accountants, doctors, lawyers and so on) have credit cards thrown at them every day through professional organisation memberships. Twice in the last 12 months I've received a 'Dear Mr Cunningham' letter, explaining that I can get a limit of $100 000—all I have to do is state that my income is above a certain level. Now that downright concerns me. Many people would find access to that kind of cash too hard to resist, which could wind them up in a lot of trouble if they're not careful.

Obviously, the real danger with credit is that we're obliged to pay the money back eventually, or should I say, we're personally liable for the debt. If we fall into trouble with repayments and can't meet our obligations, our future credit rating (serviceability assessment) may be impaired, the bank can take our assets and, in extreme instances, we can be declared bankrupt.

It's the ease of access to this sort of money that gets people in trouble. Sarah's story demonstrates the downside of over reliance on credit—not only cards, but also on personal loans—for purchasing non-income-producing assets such as furniture, fridges and TVs.

The big problem with making only the minimum payments (because that's all our disposable income allows or because that's all the institution tells us we need to repay) is that the problem compounds (compound interest's evil twin). At 20 per cent per annum, calculated *daily*, that compound effect can have a massive impact. So at the end of her finance period, Sarah still owed a lot of money on items that had depreciated. They were 'assets' in the strict sense of the word, but they weren't ever going to make her money (they weren't income producing).

One thing that catches people in this credit trap is the psychological affect credit has. There are two sides to this coin. The first is what I call the 'out of sight, out of mind' effect of credit. When we buy things on credit, there's no actual handing over of cold hard folding, so our hurt factor is greatly reduced.

For example, say I took you out on two shopping sprees—one day I put $1000 in your wallet, the next I gave you a credit card with $1000 on it. On both days, your only instructions were to buy whatever you like and to keep what you don't spend. Most people are unlikely to spend all the cash, simply because the act of parting with those crisp pineapples hurts too much, but they wouldn't blink an eye maxing out the card. (Unlike my wife, who'd spend all the cash, max out the card *and* get the card limit increased while I wasn't looking.)

It's easy to forget how much you've put on the card, especially over a month. Reality hits 30 to 55 days later when you get the statement. (Unless you're the type who doesn't even open the statement, with the philosophy of 'if a credit card statement is posted to the forest and no-one is around to open it, do I still have to pay for it?')

The second psychological affect occurs when you see the size of your debt and think 'Oh my [insert chosen deity here]—what have I done?!' Suddenly you're behind the eight ball and have to repay your debts just to get back to even. It's here that many people simply stick their head in the sand about their financial position (or undertake a course of 'retail therapy' to make themselves feel better), which only compounds the problem.

However, while there certainly are drawbacks, it's not all doom and gloom with credit cards. If you're disciplined, they can be a terrific tool in your financial armoury — but I stress, only if they're used *correctly*.

In certain circumstances, with certain cards, you can access other people's money for up to 55 days interest free and receive rewards points. These cards are great, but only if you use them in an intelligent and disciplined way.

But beware the dark side. At the time of writing, interest rates on a standard credit card are about 20 per cent per annum on purchases, and they can often be higher for cash advances. All they require is a minimum repayment every month, often as low as 5 per cent of the outstanding balance (I've seen them as low as 2 per cent). So by just paying that 5 per cent off, our credit remains intact and we still get access to money. But we're not reducing our debt — in fact, for most people it just keeps growing.

Jay's hot tip

Following are some things to consider when choosing a credit card:

- ö *Interest rate.* Generally, interest rates are relatively similar; however, watch out for the hidden and annual fees.

- ö *Interest-free period.* The longer the better. Search for a card with an interest-free period of between 40 and 55 days (I've seen them as high as six months for new customers).

- ö *Rewards points.* Some people dismiss these as a scam, but I know from experience that they really do add up. They're obviously a ploy to get you to use your card more, and that's really the only way you can get meaningful value from them. The rewards programs vary from airline tickets to whitegoods. The trick is to ensure you don't spend beyond your means and to pay off your credit card every month. Also ensure you cash in those rewards points as some companies take them off you if you don't use them.

> **Jay's hot tip** *(cont'd)*
>
> ◌ *Merchant fee.* The average merchant fee per credit card transaction (charged to the seller) is 1.5 per cent of the transaction value. Some cards are higher—for example, American Express and Diners Club. Therefore, some businesses won't accept Amex or Diners Club.

How I use credit cards

Now, this may sound hypocritical after my warnings against an over reliance on credit cards, but I put every purchase possible on plastic—groceries, dinners, whitegoods, you name it. My reasons for doing this include the following:

- With up to 55 days interest free, I can leverage (use) other people's money and put my own cash towards reducing non-tax-deductible debt, namely my mortgage (as my other debt is tax-deductible).

- There are some fantastic rewards available if you use your card enough. As mentioned earlier, with the points I accumulate (with the help of my hard-spending sweetheart), I can buy a fridge, or upgrade the whole family to business class on an overseas trip. The reason for offering these rewards is to encourage you to use your card more often. The banks are banking (as banks do) that more people than not will misuse their cards and end up paying them additional interest— that's where the discipline comes in. But if you're diligent (like me), your reward could be a trip to Noosa courtesy of the bank.

When my statement arrives each month, my wife and I grab a cuppa or a wine and read through it together. (If applicable, I also recommend you do it with your partner). As tedious as it sounds, I then categorise each transaction (by writing next to it) into groupings such as:

- entertainment (E)
- groceries (G)
- utilities (U)
- luxuries (L)

- insurance and rates (I&R)

- kids (K)

- donations (D)

- miscellaneous (M).

Yes, it's boring (and slightly nerdy), but I do it for several reasons:

- so I know how much I'm putting on credit each month, thus reducing the 'out of sight, out of mind' issue

- to ensure I pay off the required amount *on time* each month

- to rectify any errors in what I've been charged

- so I get a feel for my overall spending habits and patterns (or, should I say, *our* spending habits).

It's interesting (hey, I'm an accountant) to look at exactly how much you spend in each of these areas, just for the sheer power that comes from being aware of your spending habits (not to mention that from time to time there's a 'mystery' amount that could well be an error—and why pay for something you didn't buy?). All it takes is about 15 minutes once a month—and you'll never run the risk of getting into too much trouble.

At the end of the day, though, if you don't have the money, don't buy it! (The exception to this rule is if you're using credit to purchase an appreciating, income-generating asset.)

Jay's take aways

- In recent times, money has never been easier to get. This is good if you want to invest, but it has a downside.

- Save up before making big purchases and don't be afraid to make do until you can afford new furniture or a big-screen TV. If you don't have the cash, don't buy it!

- Understand the good and bad uses of credit.

- Beware of the 48 months interest-free trap.

- Use your cash or savings to clear non-tax-deductible debt such as a loan on your dwelling.

- Use the equity in your home to purchase income-producing assets rather than luxuries.

- Avoid any finance option that sounds too good to be true (chances are, it is). Do your own calculations and pay as much as you can each month to ensure you don't get caught with your pants down (a huge residual) at the end of the term.

- Car finance can be a good strategy provided you can claim your expenses on tax and you put the additional cash (saved from buying a car outright) towards non-tax-deductible debt (for example, towards the mortgage on your principal place of residence).

- Credit cards, used intelligently, are a powerful tool. Abuse them and pay the price (and the interest).

- Review your monthly credit card statements to monitor your spending.

Chapter 4

In the beginning, there was a budget...

> **What you'll discover in this chapter:**
>
> ☉ the three fundamental elements of any successful financial plan
>
> ☉ how (and why) to create an effective budget
>
> ☉ how to set smart goals
>
> ☉ five ways to reduce your expenses
>
> ☉ why an asset and liability statement is a crucial part of your wealth creation strategy.

A budget is the cornerstone of any wealth creation plan. It also happens to be the fourth step to getting more money in your life. Before you ramp up your investment activities, you first need to know what you've got to invest with (bearing in mind what debts you have to meet initially). Businesses couldn't operate successfully without a budget (or at least any business that's going to be around very long). Why should our personal finances be any different?

The key determinant of the amount available for your wealth creation activities is your net disposable income (NDI): your revenue, or income, minus your expenditure (including tax).

Your goal, obviously, is to get your NDI as high as possible. However, for some people (like Steve or other 'peacocks' you may know), their NDI is actually negative—they spend more than they earn.

When he first came to me, Steve had no idea that he and his wife were spending more than they earned. Despite having significant income and assets, they were spiralling into a bottomless pit of debt. How had this happened? The answer is credit. You see, banks are very generous. You only have to ring them to be offered an increase on your credit card limit. And God help you if, like Steve, you're a 'peacock' with a home loan. A redraw facility through an existing loan can be a very attractive way of getting more cash. You can redraw as much as you want, any time, up to a certain level (your pre-approved amount).

If you draw more from that redraw facility than you put in, you're actually eating into the equity in your home. And that's bad. Not only are you not paying down your home loan, in actual fact, over time your home loan will increase, which is pretty frightening. That's one of the challenges Steve and his wife faced. Their first step when addressing this problem was to prepare a household budget.

At the very least, a basic budget raises awareness of your situation. It's never pretty to stare a low or negative NDI in the face, but it's better to be aware of it rather than be an 'ostrich' and stick your head in the sand. Having an idea of what you spend your money on is very powerful—without it, you're flying blind. Bad news for any bird.

Your budget is just one part of the three-step financial plan process:

1   Identify your goals.

2   Prepare a workable, realistic and accurate budget.

3   Use your budget to create an assets and liabilities statement.

So, before you even start to think about your budget, you need to set some goals.

Identify your goals

Step one in any activity is to determine what you are trying to achieve. Whether the budget is for a business or your personal finances, start with the end in mind. If you're saving for a house, seeking to build a share portfolio or wanting to pay off credit card debt, your desired outcome will dictate the structure and focus of your budget. You also need to identify a time frame in which to achieve your objective—without this, you most likely won't reach your goal. Time frames provide an extra layer of accountability and motivation.

Sarah's goal was debt elimination. Her time frame to do this was two years after she first came to me. Steve wanted to consolidate his debt. A similar objective to Sarah, however, he at least had a portion of his debt attributable to an appreciating asset (his house). He wanted to sort out his debt and get back on a path of wealth creation rather than debt creation. Brad and Cindy's goal was to get into business and save a deposit for an investment property.

Prepare a budget

When you're ready to draw up your budget, you have two options.

The first is traditional, old school, top-down budgeting. With this type of budgeting the profit of a business or person equals their revenue less expenses. It uses last year's revenue (what you earned) to estimate what this year's revenue will be and factors in any anticipated expense increases (rarely do your expenses go down, unless that is your goal). Your estimated revenue minus your expected expenses gives you an estimated profit.

The second option, which I recommend you adopt, is bottom-up budgeting, which flips this on its head. It's a technique that's generally reserved for business owners—and if it's good enough for a business, it's good enough for my personal finances. And my clients'.

Savvy business owners begin by asking what profit level they want to achieve. They then look at last year's revenues and expenses, and determine the increase in revenue or decrease in expenses (or both) they need to achieve that profit figure.

In my humble opinion, this is the way to go for individuals who want to be fair dinkum about wealth creation. Treat your personal or family budget like that of a business, with you being the shareholder(s). But instead of profit, think in terms of net disposable income (NDI).

Your goals give you the framework to create your budget and the motivation for sticking to it. Having a specific goal, and a date by which you want to achieve that goal, gives you the incentive to save a few extra bucks or earn extra income.

Remember, bottom up. Determine the profit you want to achieve. Make sure the profit figure aligns with your goal. If your goal is to save for a $60 000 deposit on a house within a three-year time frame, and you're starting from scratch, you'll need to save $20 000 a year — your profit target.

Budgeting — the smart way

There are some important characteristics to a successful household budget. I liken them to the effective leadership skills required to run a successful business. (Yes, there I go again, bringing everything back to business. Many of you readers may not own one (yet), but if you want to take your personal finances seriously, I recommend you treat it like a business).

One of the qualities of effective leadership in business is setting *smart* goals or tasks for your team members — that is, goals that are:

- specific
- measurable
- achievable
- realistic
- timely.

Let's take a look at each of these goals in detail.

Specific goals

'Specific goals' means accurate goals. The best way to be accurate is to work out what you actually spent your money on last year — this will be the best guide to the coming year's activities. To do this effectively, review the last 12 months of bank and credit card statements. This may sound like a cumbersome process — and it is — but you need to cover every single expense that you incurred the previous year to ensure this coming budget is as accurate as possible.

In chapter 3 I outlined the benefits of reviewing your statements each month. On top of that process, you should also review all of them once a year at budget time, so you account for the year's spending.

Measurable goals

Your budget should cover 12 months, but it should also be calendarised over that period—that is, broken down into months so you can see your income and expenditure for each month. This provides several benefits.

First, you'll be prepared for fluctuations. Some months are better than others. December and January are traditionally months when we spend a lot—Christmas, New Year's, summer holidays, barbies and parties each weekend ... they all add up. You should also be aware of birthday and anniversary months, where you may want to spend up big, and of when stuff like insurances, rates and school fees are due.

Most credit card statements are issued monthly, and many people are paid monthly, so the temptation may be to simply divide your annual budget by 12. Don't! Go through your statements to identify in which months your key expenses will fall, so you can ensure you have adequate cash to get you through.

Another benefit is tracking the variance between what you budgeted for and what you've actually spent, at the end of each month (hopefully, we get some good news and come in under budget).

Achievable goals

You need to be able to stick to your budget. If you set targets you won't or can't reach, you're just setting yourself up for failure. Focus on your end goal (profit) using bottom-up budgeting and you're more likely to set an achievable budget—just ensure your profit figure is achievable, too.

Realistic goals

Where *achievable* relates to you personally, *realistic* focuses on what you've got to work with. It's not often your income will leap $100 000 in a year and your expenses rarely drop of their own accord. If your rates were $2000 last year, they're not going to halve (our councils aren't that generous). So don't strive for something that you're never going to achieve.

Timely goals

As mentioned earlier, budgets are generally created for a 12-month period. Some freaks out there may adjust their budgets biannually or quarterly. I think annually is enough. But there are circumstances, such as a new job or significant pay change, where it may be pertinent to revisit it during the year.

My advice is to tailor your budget so that any additional income contributes to your goals such as building an investment portfolio or reducing debt. When Sarah got a promotion (and a pay rise), I encouraged her to put as much as possible (no less than 80 per cent) towards reducing her debt, rather than adding to it.

Make adjustments along the way

Another characteristic of bottom-up budgeting is that the profit (or, in our case, the NDI) becomes the driver—not your income or household expenses. If you haven't achieved your desired profit after listing all your income and expenses, you can either reduce your expenses, increase your revenue or both.

The former is generally more within your control and can be achieved faster. Many people don't know how to increase their income or don't even consider it an option. That's why I've included a range of strategies to help you increase your income in chapter 5.

More often than not you will need to make adjustments to your expenses. Rarely will you just roll out last year's expenses, overlay this year's revenue and hit your profit target.

Tips to help reduce your expenses

Here are some measures I suggested Sarah and Steve take to reduce their expenditure. Enjoy.

Sarah's plan to cut back her expenses focused on eliminating her debt.

- I encouraged her to take stock of where she was at. Often, people in severe financial distress don't know exactly how much they owe and sometimes they hide from it.

- We developed a strategy of which debts to eliminate first, and contacted each of the lenders to explain Sarah's situation.

Fortunately, we were able to do some deals and negotiate a significantly lower settlement on a couple of debts.

- We worked out which 'assets' (I use the term loosely) we could sell on eBay to raise extra cash.

- We created the strictest budget *ever*, and set regular 'check-in' meetings to monitor her progress.

- She got a second job and all her additional income went to her debts.

- She increased her income by working overtime (and her hard work eventually earned her a pay rise).

Steve's steps to reduce his expenditure were mostly around considering cheaper alternatives.

- He changed from creche ($225 per week) to family day care ($45 per week—a saving of $180 per week).

- He cancelled his gym membership ($60 per month), and instead went for a run or a swim.

- Steve's wife caught the train to work to save on petrol and expensive city parking.

- Both Steve and his wife took their lunches to work.

- Using equity in his home, Steve paid off all credit card debts to eliminate the costly interest bill he'd been incurring every month.

Jay's hot tip

Here are the top five ways to reduce your expenses:

1   Visualise what your goal is for your budgeting plan. This will provide more incentive to reduce unnecessary expenses.

2   Agree with your partner about the level of rewards or wants that you have.

3   Look for an alternative to the current level of expenditure (eat out less, buy no-name brand at the supermarket, eat at Mum's twice a week ...).

The Cunningham family budget

As you might have gathered, I'm a huge wrap for a budget. Let me give you an example of how my wife, Ange, and I prepare our annual Cunningham family budget. (Two accountants under the one roof ... I know what you're thinking—what a barrel of laughs our dinner parties must be! Hey, at least they're well catered for.)

We sit down every financial year and prepare a household budget. First, we work out how much income we're going to earn for the year (the reason we start with income is because my business partner and I increase our drawings from the business each year, so the figure can vary significantly). We then ask what sort of profit we want to generate for our debt-reduction and investment strategies. Next, we determine our expenses such as the kids' schooling and sports activities, and other necessities. Finally, we work out how much we both want to spend on luxury items or wants.

Ange knows it's an annual thing, and she dreads it each year. Don't get me wrong, I don't particularly like it either; I'm not some finance freak who gets off on doing a budget. But it's crucial. Mandatory. I wouldn't be where I am financially without going through a little pain for a few hours once a year. I want to ensure we both have enough to live comfortably while still achieving our long-term wealth creation goals.

When I receive my income throughout the month, I work out exactly how much we're going to invest and divert that amount into our investment accounts. I then apportion our personal allocations—part into her account and part into mine. And, always, a little provision for a rainy day.

I never do anything half-hearted. I believe if something is worth doing, it's worth doing properly. So if you're going to do a budget, make sure you go all the way.

Sample budget planner

To give you an idea of how best to draw up your budget I've included a sample budget planner, shown in table 4.1. This is an example of the first monthly budget planner I helped Sarah develop. Using her monthly income of around $3000 as a basis, we analysed her recent spending habits to create a budget that was challenging, yet realistic. I've included suggested percentage weightings of your income next to each category so you can start thinking about your own expenditure levels.

Table 4.1: Sarah's monthly budget planner

	Percentage of income	Budgeted amount	Actual amount
Mortgage (rent)	25%	$750	$750
Groceries	25%	$750	$680
Non-income household assets (e.g. furniture)	10%	$300	$220
Entertainment	20%	$600	$400
Savings/investment	20%	$600	$950
Total	**100%**	**$3000**	**$3000**

Sarah was so determined to turn her financial fortunes around that she smashed that first budget and ended up with $350 extra savings. We then adjusted the budget to enshrine her new disciplined spending habits, thus helping her reach her goals faster.

Budgets are different for different people. There's no rule that all budgets need to be for a certain period. It depends on your circumstances and goals.

Sarah's focus was very short term (two years). Her sole purpose was to eliminate all debts. This is in contrast to Brad and Cindy, who were at a different stage in their life. They had developed a more detailed and longer term perspective (10 years) that involved accumulating income-producing assets to help with their retirement strategy.

Personally, I'm a longer term investor. My investment strategy has been structured to ensure I can achieve my goals of reducing my business's dependency on me as a salary earner and of accumulating other investments to help supplement my income, so I'm financially secure at retirement.

The 5 per cent rule

A simple, no-frills approach you can use to determine whether you will have enough in your 'asset bank' at retirement age is called the 5 per cent rule.

Divide 5 per cent into the amount of income you wish to retire on to derive the amount of assets (excluding your principal place of residence) that you need to have on retirement day.

If you wanted to retire on an income of $60 000 per annum, you would need $1.2 million ($60 000 ÷ 0.05). If your retirement number is more like $100 000, the 5 per cent rule says you'll need $2 million. It's purely a quick guide to help get you started (but as it's in today's dollars, it needs to be adjusted for CPI). When determining exactly how much money you want to retire on, I recommend you seek the advice of a quality financial adviser.

Creating an asset and liability statement

The third cog in this wheel of financial freedom is your asset and liability (A&L) statement. There's no wealth creation benefit in developing a budget that provides you with a healthy NDI if you don't have a strategy focused on either increasing assets and/or reducing liabilities. Otherwise we're likely to just throw that NDI away on wants. (This reminds me of a quote from Georgie Best, the Manchester United soccer legend: 'I spent my money on booze, birds and fast cars—the rest I just squandered'.)

Budgets should be prepared in conjunction with an A&L statement— an existing and a projected one. This is because the profit from your budget should be reflected in either an increase in your assets or a decrease in your liabilities. I stress *should be* because, as you saw in chapter 2, many people squander their profits on wants. How detailed you get at this point will depend on your circumstances.

Table 4.2 gives you an example of an asset and liability statement. You'll notice that I've helpfully suggested several categories of assets and liabilities to assist you with the process. Once completed, these categories will demonstrate if you're over or underweighted in any particular asset class. (The typical Australian investor is overweighted in residential property.) Ideally, I recommend your assets are split over at least three of the following classes, with your largest class accounting for no more than 50 per cent of the total.

Table 4.2: sample asset and liability statement

Asset	Associated liability
Home*	Home loan
Residential investment property	Investment property loans
Commercial investment property	Credit card debt
Direct shares	Personal loans
Managed investments	Margin loans
Superannuation	
Cash or fixed interest	
Business	

*Note: for wealth creation purposes, your home will not generally contribute towards increasing your financial wellbeing. Also, cars, furniture, TVs and so on are not considered income-producing assets because they don't appreciate.

Money–life balance

I'd like to mention here that life is not all about being a money guru and sticking to a financial plan. That may sound odd within the pages of a finance book, but I'm a big advocate of money–life balance. We only get one crack at life, so we should definitely enjoy it.

I tend to get a bit too excited about financial matters—not because I'm obsessed with building an empire, but because I'm genuinely passionate about the opportunities that every single person has to secure their (and their family's) financial future. Thankfully, my wife is the balancing aspect in my life. She helps me stay grounded and remember the really important things in life: family and friends.

So, to prove I'm not a boring money-freak, let me say it once and for all: we work hard to bring in income, so we should invest some for our future, use some to reduce our debt and save some for a rainy day. But we should also use some of that income to enjoy ourselves.

Jay's take aways

- A successful financial plan requires goals; a workable, realistic and accurate budget; and an assets and liabilities statement.

- A budget is the cornerstone of any wealth creation plan — you first need to know what you've got to play with.

- Your net disposable income (revenue less expenditure) determines your wealth creation activities.

- Use bottom-up budgeting. Work out your profit first, then review your revenue and expenses to determine what needs to change.

- Always strive for a money–life balance.

- Make your budget *smart* — specific, measurable, achievable, realistic, timely.

- You'll need to make adjustments to your income or (more likely) to your expenses.

- Five ways to reduce your expenses:
  - visualise your goal for your budgeting plan
  - determine the level of rewards or wants you will allow yourself
  - look for cheaper alternatives
  - get a good accountant and maximise your tax deductions
  - take excess money off yourself, so you can't spend it.

- A wealth creation plan needs a budget prepared in conjunction with an assets and liability statement.

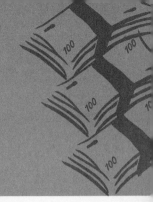

Chapter 5

Workin' hard for the money

What you'll discover in this chapter:

ŏ   the four ways we all make money

ŏ   the four things that every business has in common—know these, and you can impress any boss

ŏ   why you should put in hard at work

ŏ   seven things you can do to make more money (none of which will land you in a cell with a roommate called Bubba)

ŏ   the concept of leverage—the key to fast-tracking your wealth creation plan.

The most common question I'm asked is: 'How do I make money?' (usually followed by 'Fast'). Everyone wants to learn about a get-rich-quick scheme. Understandably, too. Who wouldn't be interested in hearing about a secret way to make cash that nobody else has heard of?

I'll tell you who: accountants. We know that there's no such thing. Well, not in the sense that everyone else thinks. You see, we accountants look at the big picture. For us, two years can be considered quick—if you're talking in terms of a 10- or 20-year wealth creation strategy.

So, wanna know how to make money fast (in accountant-time)? Well, you've come to the right book. Maximising your income-earning potential is the fifth step on the road to wealth.

There are four ways to make money:

◙   working (what accountants call personal exertion)

- buying property

- buying shares

- buying a business.

This chapter focuses on the first (and most common) way — generating the most money from your job. You may have already bought property or shares, or be ready to buy a business. But whatever your situation, there are gems a-plenty in the coming pages, so I encourage you to read on — treat this chapter as a refresher. Oh, and start looking for a bigger wallet.

Personal exertion — the first way most of us get more cash

Personal exertion is fancy accounting terminology for working. It's getting paid for your time. It's how most of us earn the majority of our income and the most popular way to get more money. It's easy, simple and doesn't necessarily require too much strategic thought. Nor is there much risk associated with it (but that generally means low returns). Instead of investing money for a return, we're investing our precious time and effort. Making more money through personal exertion generally involves *working harder* — getting a promotion, a second job and working overtime.

The reason so many of us rely on personal exertion to increase our disposable income is the same thing that holds most people back in life: fear. It's fear that prevents us from achieving what we want in life — whether that be fear of failure or fear of success. When it comes to money, our fear of losing it can lead us to take no action, but there's still a risk in doing nothing.

As I've mentioned, investing in the sharemarket and businesses, in particular, and property to a lesser extent, carry risks that just aren't applicable to working. But you won't get to where you want by playing it totally safe. As you'll discover in later chapters the benefits of taking calculated risks really make property, shares and business ownership attractive options.

Benefits of putting in at work

When it comes to making money, most of us have that 'put your head down and work harder' mentality ingrained in us, because that's what our parents did. Sure, we need to look beyond our upbringing to find other ways to supplement this hard work, but I wholeheartedly encourage you to put in extra at work so you can get ahead. Now before you accuse me of contradicting myself, I ask you to stay with me — this is just one part of a long and winding financial journey.

Working hard brings many benefits — not just the financial benefits of getting a promotion (and thus a pay rise), but also the psychological benefits associated with being recognised for what you do and being good at it. That sense of achievement makes you feel better about yourself.

The other benefit of a promotion is that your colleagues change. You generally interact with workers at your level, so if you become a manager, you end up spending time with other managers. Typically, these people are savvier with their money, so the old adage 'you become who you associate with' means you could potentially go from someone who lives from pay cheque to pay cheque to someone who earns more income and has a financial plan in place.

Getting a pay rise increases your disposable income. This increase should allow you to participate in various investment opportunities, which I'll take you through in later chapters. However, you need to be disciplined and use the additional income for good.

Finally, why wouldn't you want to excel at your job and be recognised at your workplace? Why wouldn't you want to be good at what you do? Usually, it doesn't require a big commitment or huge effort to go from a mediocre performer to somebody who excels at their job. By excelling, there are so many opportunities that are available to you. So the next question is: how do we excel at work?

Ways to excel at work

There are several ways to excel at work. To get ahead you need to both understand the four pillars of business, and show that you want to learn and move up in the company.

Understand the four pillars of business

Although all jobs appear vastly different on the surface, the core activities of each business—and to some extent, the jobs we do in that business—are the same. Every business that I've worked with (and I've been advising business owners for 11 years now) has four common pillars or principles: people, processes, customers and financials.

If you take the time to understand the make-up of these four pillars in your business, you'll be more aware of opportunities to add real value to the organisation and thus be considered an asset by your employer. It will also give your employer confidence in your ability to step up and assume more responsibility. (I take a closer look at the four pillars in chapter 10.)

Show that you're interested

It's those qualities mentioned previously that I look for in our team at The Practice. It's not necessarily the most talented that succeed, but, rather, those with the impetus to succeed. The cynical may say it's the *perception* that becomes reality—if your managers think you're working hard, then in their minds, you are. But as managers, that's quite often all you have to go on—your perception of people. Even if you don't have a lot of self-confidence, you can improve your standing at work just by doing the right things.

But enough about you ...

It's this drive that helped me get ahead at my first full-time job, which was at Ford Motor Company, where I stayed for four years. Despite being a short period of time in the overall scheme of things, those four years gave me the skill set and the impetus to establish my own firm, and a lot of the practices and methodologies that we use today at The Practice have been adopted from that mighty blue oval.

I had the opportunity to learn from some great minds, particularly the managers that I worked with. But it was from the company's dedication to excellence that I was able to derive many benefits.

Firstly, earning more money meant I could save more and set aside a nest egg to invest in the working capital of that business when I was ready to take the plunge.

Secondly, I made many great friends and influential contacts, people such as vice presidents, who played a significant role down the track when I was building my business. I'm proud to say that many of those executives are now clients of mine.

Thirdly, I got to learn about the business at Ford, and that all businesses are built on those same four pillars. I was able to take that understanding of how that organisation ran and use it as the blueprint for developing my own business.

Finally, I felt good about myself. I gained confidence from knowing that I was good at what I did. More importantly, I also knew that I had developed a very important skill—the ability to learn—and I was able to use that ability (which we can all achieve) to become great at something.

How did I implement my learning skills at Ford? I asked questions. I learned what the business did and, no matter how insignificant my role was, how my role added value to the business. In that first year, I used to grab a quick bite and spend the rest of my lunchtimes wandering through the factory floor asking the managers questions—just to gain a greater understanding of what the company did.

I remember some advice one of my mentors—the vice president of finance, Paul Lewis—gave me in my final year: 'Well, Jason, it doesn't matter if you don't show up tomorrow, we're still going to build 440 Falcons'. That was a really important lesson for me. Despite how important I thought my role in finance was (and how important I thought *I* was), at the end of the day the business is about making and selling cars. It made me appreciate the big picture and my position in the larger scheme of things. This lesson would stand me in good stead not only in work, but in life.

Not only did I learn by asking questions, I also showed my managers that I *wanted* to learn and that I wanted to contribute. It's these qualities that encouraged my managers to promote me and put me in a position where I was successful at work, which led to me earning more money than my peers.

What to do if you can't get ahead

There are occasions or situations or employers where, no matter how hard you try, how much you get involved or how many questions you ask, they are simply too narrow-minded and you don't get the opportunity to improve your position at work. In those situations, you're left with two options should you want to increase the amount of money you earn:

- *Leave the organisation.* In 2008 Australia's unemployment rate hovered at around the 4 per cent mark, meaning there were almost more job vacancies than people to fill them. So, if you're good at what you do, present yourself well, your resume stacks up and you keep trying with interviews, you shouldn't have a problem getting a job at an organisation that values contributors.

- *Get a second job.* Sure, you have to put in a few extra hours, but if you can get up an hour earlier or spend an hour less watching TV, and be paid for six or seven additional hours a week, that can really help kick-start your savings plan. Many people are deterred by the notion of getting a second job due to the tax implications, but this is a misnomer: you don't pay any extra tax, you just don't have the benefit of the tax-free threshold for that second job. You'll pay more tax up-front, but get it back when you file your tax return.

Whether you get a new job, a promotion or a second job, if you implement the practices discussed in this chapter you should discover:

- increased confidence and, therefore, self-belief
- a sense of belonging and contribution to the team
- an increase in income.

That increase in income should lead to an increased net disposable income (provided you are mindful of the 'more you earn, the more you spend' phenomenon discussed in chapter 1). You can then use that increased cash flow to form the basis of your savings plan. Over the next few chapters we'll look at some opportunities to invest those savings, whether that be property, the sharemarket or a business.

But before we get ahead of ourselves, let's first look at some other ways you can get more cash in your life.

Practical ways to get more cash

Don't be afraid to say it—you want more cash. And I'm here to show you how to get it. Let's take a look at some of the strategies I helped Sarah use to increase her disposable income.

There are seven things Sarah did to get more cash (most of which I encouraged her to do):

- change industry
- keep seeking opportunities for a pay rise
- take on part-time work
- strive to achieve bonuses
- study to improve her income-earning prospects
- sell stuff
- find a good accountant and financial planner.

Change industry

When I first met Sarah, she'd already made the big change from hairdressing to administration within the finance industry. There's absolutely nothing wrong with hairdressing as a profession; Sarah had decided of her own accord that she had a better earning potential if she moved into the finance sector and was prepared to work hard to rise through the ranks.

Changing industry or profession alone won't fix your money woes. You often need to take a step backwards when you shift because you may not have many skills or much experience in the new sector. In cases like this, you'll need to utilise all the tips I've provided in this chapter to get the most out of your new industry.

Keep seeking opportunities for a pay rise

Sarah was dedicated to continually seeking promotion opportunities with her new employer. This doesn't mean she started stabbing people in the back with the sole objective of climbing the corporate ladder; she simply worked hard, impressed her bosses with her dedication and commitment, and demonstrated her readiness to take the next step. Consequently, she moved from administration to accounting, with a handy pay rise for her troubles.

Take on part-time work

Don't be afraid to trade off some of that valuable TV-watching time in order to generate additional income. Sarah did some hairdressing on weekends to supplement her income and help her achieve her debt-reduction goals faster. You'd be surprised how just a few hours a week (either after-hours or on the weekend) can help get a savings plan kick-started.

Strive to achieve bonuses

Sarah was lucky enough to be working for an exceedingly generous boss (me) who incentivised his team with bonus opportunities for client referrals and cross-sales (for example, encouraging a client to take up a financial services product). Sarah made the most of these opportunities. She took the time to understand what the organisation was all about—that is, getting clients, retaining them with great service and educating them about other products that may be of benefit to them—and learning how she could be of most value to the organisation. She enjoyed a 10 per cent bonus for her troubles.

Study to improve income-earning prospects

As with most people who change careers, Sarah started at the bottom. By studying and gaining qualifications, she not only boosted her short-term earning capacity, but also ensured she could take advantage of future promotion opportunities.

Sell stuff

Once she acknowledged that she was living beyond her means, Sarah was better able to see the difference between her wants and her needs. The first step was to sell her car and catch public transport—environmental concerns (helped along by rising petrol prices) are making this a necessary course of action for many people. Sarah also sold some of her possessions on eBay. The proceeds of these sales (and her car expense savings) helped eat into her debt and increase her weekly savings amount.

Find a good accountant and financial planner

Didn't Sarah luck out here—she found me! Even if you're not so fortunate, finding a good accountant and financial adviser will help you plan your wealth creation strategy and maximise your current situation.

Using leverage to fast-track your wealth creation plan

After you've worked on increasing your income through personal exertion, the next way to boost your income is through using leverage. Investing in property, shares or a business all allow you to use leverage. You don't necessarily need to use leverage; you can always use your own money. But leverage is the key to fast-tracking your wealth creation strategy.

So, what is leverage? Leverage is a term used to define the use of other people's money or time to maximise your return on an investment or activity. From an investment perspective it can be seen as the use of credit or borrowed money to increase your capacity to invest and thus increase the rate of return from that investment—for example, buying shares using a margin loan or purchasing an investment property with a home loan.

Leverage is something that Michael Gerber (author of *The E-Myth*) and Robert Kiyosaki (author of *Rich Dad, Poor Dad* and *The Cashflow Quadrant*) refer to repeatedly as a key wealth creation mechanism. They both believe that the only way to make real money is through using leverage. And, dear reader, as I'll reveal through the next few chapters, I agree.

Following are the different types of leverage that we're going to explore in chapters 6 to 10:

◙ using other people's money (mainly the bank's) to enable us to enter the property and stock markets

◙ using other people's time—this relates to business investment.

When considering your options for using leverage, you'll see that running a business is not for everyone. It takes a certain breed of person. But we all have the ability to use leverage investment strategies to enter the property and stock markets.

Jay's take aways

- There are four main ways to make money: personal exertion, and investing in property, shares and a business.

- Personal exertion is the easiest way to make more money. No strategic thought is required and there is no risk—but the returns are low.

- Fear is the biggest factor holding people back in life—free yourself from it, by allowing yourself to make mistakes (and forgiving yourself when you do), and you'll really start to go places.

- The benefits of putting in more at work include:
  - being good at what you do and getting recognised for the work you do
  - getting promoted
  - an increase in disposable income (through a pay rise)
  - a sense of achievement, which makes you feel better about yourself
  - mixing with managers who are typically savvier with their money.

- Understand the four pillars of business—people, processes, customers and financials—and you understand the fundamental drivers of any business. Focusing on these areas in your work will add value to your role and impress any boss.

- Ask questions. Not only will you learn about the business and your role in it, it demonstrates that you're keen and want to contribute.

- It's not necessarily the most talented that succeed, but rather those with the impetus to succeed. Perception equals reality.

- Increase your disposable income by:
  - changing industries or professions
  - seeking pay rises through promotions, added responsibility or new tasks
  - looking for bonuses—either through an official bonus structure or through above-average performance
  - getting some part-time work
  - studying to improve your income-earning prospects
  - selling stuff
  - finding a good accountant and financial planner.
- Leverage (other people's money or time) allows us to build up and fast-track our investment portfolio.

Chapter 6

Your home is your castle – and your cash cow

> **What you'll discover in this chapter:**
>
> ♂ why property is such a fantastic investment
>
> ♂ the changing face of property ownership and loan structures
>
> ♂ what equity is and how you can use it to fast-track your financial plan
>
> ♂ the difference between purchasing a home and an investment property
>
> ♂ renting versus buying.

Looking back to when I was growing up—somewhere between the 'dark ages' (when we only had black and white TV in the '70s) and the Jurassic (Park) period (the early '90s)—I still can't believe how much things have changed. In 1975 my folks bought their first house in suburban Melbourne for $25 000. Today there are TVs worth more than that! Despite the differences in house prices, incomes and haircuts, there are still some valuable lessons we can learn from the baby boomers in terms of their attitude to credit and savings. At the same time, however, there are several reasons to challenge entrenched notions of property as our main (or sole, excluding super) investment strategy.

The times have a-changed

Thirty years ago attitudes to purchasing property were a lot different from that of first-home buyers today. My parents borrowed only 50 per cent of the purchase price—meaning they actually *saved* for a *50 per cent deposit* (some readers may need to look up those 's' and 'd' words in the dictionary). Their sole focus then was to pay off their home loan as fast as they could. So we had milk crates for furniture until they could afford to buy a lounge suite. Don't get me wrong, we didn't eat gruel for dinner, but Mum and Dad, and people of their era, understood and lived the concept of delayed gratification. They worked hard (sometimes a couple of jobs) to pay down the loan, *then* bought wants such as furniture, holidays and things for the kids. They waited until they could afford it.

This attitude is not for everyone. In this chapter I'll discuss some of the various home finance options available depending on your situation—whether you're a first-home buyer or an investor, the size of your deposit and your ability to pay off the mortgage, to name a few. In fact, buying property is the sixth step to getting more money in your life, and in chapters 7 and 8, I'll examine a range of wealth creation strategies using equity in your property. While seemingly quaint and old-fashioned, I believe there's definitely some merit in the baby boomers' dedication to releasing the mortgage noose from around their necks.

We also need to acknowledge that it's much easier to obtain credit these days, whether that be home loans, personal loans or credit cards. Our parents practically had to name their first born after their bank manager to ensure they could get a loan—these days, the banks come to your house to offer to lend you money. Why the dramatic shift? It's largely due to the deregulation of the financial sector, which has led to increased competition among financial institutions. Banks have had to become more proactive in maintaining their market share against aggressive and nimble new competitors. As their ever-increasing profits show, lending is obviously very good for business.

These forces have seen lending institutions continually drop their lending criteria. Some lenders now assess pre-tax rather than net (after-tax) income, meaning more clients are eligible for loans. Many offer low-doc or no-doc loans, so you can access considerable credit without providing any proof of your ability to repay it, purely so more people can take out loans. Later in the chapter I'll discuss the impact of less stringent lending requirements in the personal loan sector.

Types of home loans

The property-purchasing mindset of our generation (x, y, π — whatever we are) has taken on a whole new outlook. As table 6.1 shows, home loans and the way we use them have also changed. Long gone is the good old principal-and-interest loan. More and more homebuyers (and property investors) are taking out 25- to 30-year interest-only loans and don't really have the focus that our parents did to pay down those loans as quickly as possible. Today, the aim is to get in there and buy a house *right now*, and keep up with the Joneses while we're at it, decking the house out in the latest designer furniture (when was the last time you saw a new homeowner 'making do' with old furniture or an old telly?).

Table 6.1: comparison of home loan characteristics, 1975 and 2008

	My parents' home loan in 1975	The average Aussie loan in 2008
Property value	$25000	$450000
Deposit saved	$12250 (50%)	$45000 (10%)
Loan value	$12250	$405000
Type of loan	Principal and interest	Interest only
Furniture and fittings	Preloved	Topnotch
Time taken to pay off loan	15 years	Will it ever get paid off?

There are also other new types of loans such as redraw facilities and offset accounts. Now, don't get me wrong; if these are used correctly, they can be a very powerful tool in a wealth creation strategy. However, if using these facilities for wants (luxuries) rather than needs, this misuse can be to the detriment of the average person.

All too often I see young clients who have borrowed 90 or 95 per cent of the value of the home, getting interest-only loans and just servicing the interest, rather than focusing on chewing into the principal. After a couple of years the value of the property has gone through the roof (as it did in the 2000s), therefore, the equity in their home has increased, so they celebrate by borrowing *more* money against their home, through redraw facilities, to deck it out with furniture. The problem is that the value of their debt is increasing, but not necessarily the value of their income-producing asset (your dwelling is an asset, but it doesn't generate income—unless someone is living with you and paying rent).

Modern homeownership hurdles

Things are certainly different from my parents' day. Society has changed, for good and for not-so-good. I'll tell you one thing—next time your parents start banging on about the 'good old days' and how much better things used to be, you can agree with them on one point—buying property was a hell of a lot easier!

The obvious advantage for baby boomers was the lower cost of property back then and the reduced on-costs of purchasing property such as stamp duty and lenders mortgage insurance (LMI). At the time of writing, stamp duty in Victoria was 6.25 per cent of the purchase price on anything above $100 000—so stamp duty on a $500 000 property was around $25 000. The stamp duty for my parents' property in 1975 was under $1000. A big difference. (See chapter 7 for a complete list of stamp duty rates.)

These low costs are in contrast to the early 2000s, where we've just come out of one of the biggest property booms on record. Obviously income levels have also increased in relative dollar terms, but there's no denying the significant hurdles facing property buyers these days.

The property boom has been exceedingly kind to the baby boomers. Let's suppose my mum and dad live in their first home for the rest of their life. In 2008 the value of that $25 000 property is the best part of $900 000. They've paid the home off and what they've now got is access to equity. They can use this equity in their existing property as leverage to help them purchase other income-producing assets (such as an investment property or shares). The bank can use some of this equity as security to reduce their risk, meaning they're prepared to lend them additional money.

So what does the future hold for property? No-one has a crystal ball to predict what will happen—although it's hard to see how property could continue to increase at the rates it has in the last decade. It may well do so, particularly in sought-after areas, but it's prudent to expect some dampening of growth levels. In early 2008 the International Monetary Fund (IMF) released its *World Economic Outlook*, in which it listed Australia as having one of the four most overvalued housing markets in the Western world and one of the four highest levels of housing debt.[1] The IMF estimated that Australian housing prices in 2007 were 25 per cent higher than could be explained by economic fundamentals. It recognised that this may reflect factors not included in its modelling, but nevertheless there remained a risk of a sharp correction.

Is the great Aussie dream still relevant?

We need to ask ourselves if owning our own home is as important to us as it was 30 years ago. If I were to buy the same property today that my folks did (for $900 000) and pay that loan off by retirement age (60), I'd have a couple of things:

- a roof over my head
- an asset that I own outright
- a stoop from all the hard work I've been doing to pay the loan off over 25 years.

So after all my toil, I'd have a valuable asset, sure, but not an income-producing asset (remember, your home is not an income-producing asset, unless you receive rent). To realise my asset, I'd have to sell my house. I'd make a tidy profit based on my original purchase price, but I still need somewhere to live—it's this next purchase that can so often cancel out any gains made on your sale, as the price rises that generated your profit apply in reverse when you buy your next property.

---

1 T Colebatch, 'Australia vulnerable to US "tsunami", IMF warns', *The Age*, 9 April 2008, <www.theage.com.au>.

To make that first home a worthwhile investment, I'd need to buy a smaller house with the funds from the sale of the property so that I can make a profit on the transactions (thankfully I'm 60 and want to downsize). I can then use the difference as an investment to live off.

Rather than buy another place of residence, I could have used those funds to purchase an income-producing asset. Sure I'd have to rent, but siphoning an equivalent mortgage repayment amount towards the purchase of an income-producing asset, such as a business or share portfolio, can be a very effective investment strategy.

Alternatively I could buy two smaller properties (around $500 000 each), live in one and rent the other out (so it becomes an income-generating asset).

Even though homeownership may seem out of reach for many these days, with a little know-how you can still live the great Aussie dream (something I take a closer look at in chapter 7).

Is property the right investment for you?

Do you have a heartbeat? Then, *yes*, property is the right investment for you.

Property is cool. It's a lot like charisma, or talent: you've either got it, or you don't. Those already in the market talk about their property like a child, telling everyone who'll listen that they just *have* to do it. Those that don't own property, and with each passing day feel the prospect slipping further away, justify it by saying they prefer the flexibility, freedom and carefree nature of renting—or that they're lying in wait for the market to drop.

Before I shoot those arguments down in flames, let me disclose that I'm a property owner. In fact, I own (or am in the process of owning) four. I don't tell you this to brag; just to demonstrate that I'm fully committed to what I'm about to tell you.

The great thing about property as an investment is that we've all lived in a house, a flat or an apartment at some stage, so we all have a basic understanding of what property is. And, typically, if you understand something, you're more likely to (a) overcome your fear and get involved, and (b) be successful at it. This goes a long way to explaining property's popularity as an investment vehicle for most Australians—unlike hedged funds, we all understand what we're investing in. We feel comfortable with solid, tangible bricks and mortar as part of our investment strategy.

Following are some of the benefits of investing in property:

- Rather than pay off someone else's mortgage through renting, you can live in your own home and pay off *your* mortgage.

- In the eyes of the banks, property is second to cash as the most secure asset. It's nowhere near as volatile as the sharemarket. For this reason, lenders typically feel more comfortable lending money to purchase property rather than shares or other investments.

- Buying a property and owning it by the time you retire enables you to live off a lesser amount in retirement, as you don't need to service a loan or pay rent. The average householder spends about one-third of his or her household income on rent, and even more (up to 40 per cent) when repaying mortgages. If this is paid off come retirement time, it's a huge strain off your retirement income.

- Your house can act as an emergency fund. I don't recommend you do this, but at least you have the option to scale down in retirement. You can sell your house, buy a smaller one and put the difference into super or another income-producing asset or investment should the need arise. This strategy is also used by many older Australians to fund a move into a retirement village. But I stress, you're far better to plan ahead so you can still enjoy a rental income stream if possible.

- Although past returns are not necessarily an indication of future returns, the independent real estate information house RESIDEC estimates that for the period 1983 to 2008, the average Sydney house value has increased by more than 620 per cent. Brisbane and Melbourne have done even better (or worse, depending on which side of the homeownership divide you dwell in)—up by a staggering 720 per cent and 800 per cent respectively. They're incredible returns in 25 years.

  The value of a property purchased in a good area is likely to significantly increase. And the benefit here is that by purchasing your own home, you get the opportunity to use any increase in equity in that property as security for future investments—whether that's an additional property, or investing in the sharemarket or a business.

- You can take advantage of the tax benefits offered to property investors. Negative gearing allows investors to offset any losses arising from your investment property against other income that you earn, so that your overall tax burden is reduced. While a rental property provides income in the form of rent, you also incur costs such as interest on your investment property loan, real estate agent expenses and depreciation. With negative gearing, you can subtract these costs from your rental income. The net loss on that property can then be used to offset the income that you receive from your employer (thus reducing your overall taxable income). Any tax you have paid that's in excess of what you actually owe is refunded to you. If you manage your money effectively, that refund can be used to fund another investment or, at the very least, be used to pay down some of the principal of your loan.

Should you rent or buy?

Everyone's circumstances are different, so you need to see an adviser for advice that is best for you; however, in my experience, there are only a couple of situations where it would be pertinent to rent instead of buy.

The first relates to professional stock market traders. I have clients and friends who actively buy and sell shares over the short term for profit. They require large sums of capital to trade the market effectively. Rather than tie up their cash in a huge non-income-producing asset like a house, they're better using that capital to buy and sell shares. They make fantastic returns, so the strategy of renting rather than buying makes sense for them.

The second situation is when your future is uncertain. You may have moved into an area that is foreign to you for a short period of time, with the expectation that you'll move again in a year or two. Rather than locking up your capital in an area you have no knowledge of, it may be better to rent. Entry costs are high, so it pays for first-home buyers to know about the area they're looking to invest in. A good friend of mine moved to Alice Springs for work—he had no idea how long he would be there and actually ended up staying several years. But his strategy of renting rather than buying within his first two years was the safe, smart way to go.

Take a long-term view

With all investments, timing is everything. This is more pronounced with property—the natural tendency is to be guided by the state of the market. If prices are going up, we are encouraged to make an investment as we can see growth. If prices rise too much, we hold off until the cycle shifts. The opposite holds true if the market is in decline, although there is a real incentive to snag a bargain. But I want you to be thinking less about timing your entry point and more about time *in* the market—the number of years you remain in the investment.

Remember, your investment goal should be primarily to secure your retirement. Most of us have until age 65 to reach that goal, giving us somewhere between 20 to 40 years in the market. This sort of time frame makes it easy to weather any turbulence in the property market.

This book doesn't set out to show you how to build a multimillion-dollar property portfolio. I'll leave that to the property experts such as Steve McKnight (author of *From 0 to 130 Properties in 3.5 Years* and *From 0 to 260+ Properties in 7 Years*). My aim is to show you how to make the most of what you've got. And I'm a firm believer that *anybody* can become financially secure if they adopt the strategies that I outline.

Jay's take aways

- Home loans and the way we use them have changed. We've gone from principal-and-interest to interest-only loans, with additions such as redraw facilities and offset accounts.
- Avoid the temptation of dipping into the equity in your home for wants.
- Most people are better off buying rather than renting.

■ The benefits of investing in property include:

    ▫ we all need somewhere to live—you may as well pay off your own mortgage rather than someone else's (by renting)

    ▫ property is a secure asset for leverage purposes

    ▫ owning your property come retirement lets you live off a lesser amount in retirement

    ▫ your house is an emergency fund

    ▫ the tax breaks (negative gearing)

    ▫ excellent potential returns—house values have risen by up to 800 per cent over 25 years in some states.

Chapter 7

Getting into the property market

What you'll discover in this chapter:

ŏ how the banks assess your loan worthiness

ŏ which type of loan is right for you

ŏ home purchase strategies, and how an offset account can boost your property purchasing power

ŏ the six things to do before taking the property plunge

ŏ how you can own not one, but *two* properties—outright—before you retire.

Okay, Jay, sounds great. I'm going once...twice...sold on the property thing. So how do I get amongst it?

In chapter 6 I explained why you should get into the property market. In this chapter, I give you the steps to do it.

Getting started

The starting point for most of us is our first home. Regardless of whether you're buying the property yourself or engaging a professional to help with the purchase (such as a licensed real estate agent or buyers' advocate), there are a number of boxes I recommend you tick before acquiring your first home (or any subsequent properties for that matter). They include:

- conduct market research

- save for a deposit

- work out how much you can borrow

- understand which type of loan is right for you

- get the right ownership structure

- read (and understand) the fine print.

Let's take a look at each of these in turn.

Conduct market research

It's vital to have an understanding of property values in different areas before you make a purchase. If going it alone, I recommend attending a few auctions beforehand and practise bidding, because believe you me, putting your hand up at an auction to make your first purchase is downright scary, particularly in front of a big crowd. Be prepared for a serious adrenaline rush. What would your biggest purchase decision have been to date? A car, perhaps? Now times that stress by 100 — and for good measure, make the decision *on the spot*, with a bunch of strangers trying to outbid you and an auctioneer trying to suck even more money out of you.

Practice makes perfect. Try opening up the bidding on a house you've done some research on. You should have a fair idea of the reserve, so you should be safe. Be careful, however, as there are no cooling off periods at auctions. Man, what a rush!

If you don't have the time to practise-bid or you just aren't comfortable putting your hand up at an auction, you can use a buyer's advocate — that is, pay a fee to have someone else purchase a property on your behalf. The theory is that because buyers' advocates are experienced in purchasing property, they'll be well placed to get you the best deal available. Another strategy is to get a close friend to bid on your behalf. The beauty of this is that it takes the emotion out of the bidding process and purchasing decision — your proxy has clearly established parameters that he or she will stay within (unlike you).

Save for a deposit

It's essential to save for a deposit. Your deposit not only needs to cover the property price, it must also factor in the many other acquisition costs. These include stamp duty, paying for any rates (such as council and water) that have been paid in advance by the previous owner, title office fees, conveyancing, solicitor fees and mortgage registration costs. Your deposit needs to account for 20 per cent of the purchase price plus these additional costs, otherwise you will be charged lenders mortgage insurance (LMI)—something I take a closer look at later in the chapter.

Work out how much you can borrow

You *must* establish how much you can borrow before auction day. In some states there's no cooling-off period, so if you put your hand up, and it stays up when the music stops, that property is yours. If you can't come good with the cash to honour your purchase, chances are you'll lose your deposit. (When purchasing a property via private sale, you can make an offer 'subject to finance'—meaning should you not be successful in gaining finance, you can pull out of the deal and not lose your deposit.)

There are two ways to work out how much you can borrow—have a meeting with your bank or see a mortgage broker. I recommend the latter. Mortgage brokers are not biased towards one bank, which means you should be able to get the best deal going. Most have a panel of up to 30 lenders for you to choose from. They can also help you work out the best option for your needs. When your bank or mortgage broker confirms how much you can borrow, this is called pre-approval. For a guide, check out the very cool mortgage calculator at <www.wheresmymoney.com.au>.

Understand which type of loan is right for you

The different types of loans available are covered later in the chapter, but ensure you seek the advice of a professional prior to jumping in. There's no crime in spending a few hours with an accountant, financial adviser or mortgage broker—he or she can help you to avoid an expensive mistake.

Get the right ownership structure

There are legal and financial implications for the ownership structure of a property (such as asset protection). It's important to understand and consider your options. You can buy a property in your name, your spouse's name, in joint names with your spouse, or in the name of a company or trust. The various options are outlined in chapter 11, but, again, seek the advice of a professional.

Read (and understand) the fine print

When you buy a property (especially your first home), the additional costs of entering the property market are extremely high—particularly stamp duty and other costs, such as land tax, and adjustments such as conveyancing (changing the title from the previous owner to your name). Table 7.1 lists the stamp duty rates across Australia.

Table 7.1: stamp duty rates across Australia based on a $500 000 property (effective August 2008)

State	Stamp duty payable on a $500 000 property
Australian Capital Territory	$20 500
New South Wales	$17 994
Northern Territory	$23 929
Queensland	$8 750
South Australia	$21 330
Tasmania	$17 550
Victoria	$25 070
Western Australia	$19 665

Jay's hot tip

For up-to-date information on stamp duty rates in your neck of the woods, go to the relevant State Revenue Office or visit <www.wheresmymoney. com.au>.

What type of loan should I choose?

As you consider the plethora of loan structures available today, you should take into account the following factors:

- your reasons for the purchase—buying a dwelling that you'll live in versus buying an investment property
- the percentage of the property's value you are borrowing
- your available cash flow
- your ability to meet your repayment obligations if something unforeseen happens.

Typically, your first (and for many people, only) purchase will be a dwelling to live in, with perhaps an investment property after that. Homebuyers who intend to live in the dwelling (called a principal place of residence) usually favour a principal-and-interest (P&I) loan, while people purchasing an investment property generally choose an interest-only (IO) loan. The reason for this is that unlike home loan debt, the debt associated with an investment property is tax-deductible. It makes sense, therefore, to pay off your home loan principal first, as you can at least get a tax break for your investment property loan costs. However, if you have the available cash flow, it may be worth going with a P&I loan for both.

If you have to use an IO loan, I recommend what I do myself: take out an IO loan with an offset account, where all your interest payments are made against the loan and any principal amounts are paid into the offset account. This then gives you the flexibility to access equity in the property (via the offset account) without having to reapply for finance through the bank's regular channels.

But be warned: this strategy should be used only by disciplined investors—that is, those who will continually pay into the offset account (even though not required to) and who won't access the funds to purchase non–income-producing assets ('wants' or 'luxuries').

There are many strategies to help you purchase your home, such as:

- *taking out an interest-only loan, with no expectation to repay the principal.* The assumption here (and it is a brave one) is that the property will appreciate more than your principal amount, so you need only worry about the interest, and you will eventually be able to sell the property, pay back the principal and pocket a profit for your risk.

- *taking out an interest-only loan for a short period (one to three years).* Some homebuyers start out with an IO loan with a view to reverting to a PI loan when their circumstances change. They may anticipate getting a pay rise or are waiting for a spouse to return to work after maternity or paternity leave.

Risk and serviceability

When you apply for a loan, there are two criteria the banks use to assess your loan worthiness—risk (security) and serviceability.

Banks have a standard level of risk they are prepared to take when lending money (their standard position). The usual level of exposure they are prepared to risk for residential properties is 80 per cent of the property's value.

The serviceability criterion relates to your (perceived) ability to meet your monthly repayment obligations. This is based on factors such as:

- your income
- type of employment (casual work and low-paid professions, and, in certain circumstances, being self-employed, will work against you here)
- your employment history
- any other income-producing assets you may have.

We can learn from the banks here—it's important for us to consider our ability to repay the loan, which we eventually have to do, taking into account potential unforeseen circumstances. These can include interest rate rises (between 2007 and 2008 interest rates went from 6 per cent to 9 per cent, but since then have been falling), being laid off, or, touch wood, significant injury or illness.

Lenders mortgage insurance

The price of property has skyrocketed (granted, so too have our incomes). This increase, coupled with the easier availability of credit and our changing attitudes to saving, mean it is not uncommon for people to borrow 80, 90, even *over 100 per cent* of a property's value. However, when borrowing more than 80 per cent, you're required to pay lenders mortgage insurance (LMI), which is basically an insurance policy that you pay for on the bank's behalf, to protect the bank against any exposure from their standard lend position.

LMI is calculated as a percentage of the total loan size — around 1.25 per cent. Table 7.2 shows the LMI you would be liable for if you borrowed 90 per cent of a $500 000 property.

Table 7.2: LMI amount for a loan of 90 per cent of a $500 000 property

Property value	$500 000
Bank's preferred exposure amount (80%)	$400 000
Actual amount borrowed (90%)	$450 000
Difference (unacceptable exposure component)	$50 000
LMI rate* (at 1.25% of the total loan size)	$5 625

*Note: the LMI rate may differ between lenders depending on their insurer and the relevant policy or criteria.

Therefore, when borrowing more than 80 per cent of a property's value, you need to save for a 20 per cent deposit *plus* additional costs (LMI, stamp duty, legals and adjustments).

As table 7.3 (overleaf) demonstrates, additional costs can really add up and put you at risk of incurring LMI. Do your sums to ensure these costs don't push you over the LMI limit.

There are two reasons you should try to avoid incurring LMI. The first, and most obvious, is the additional cost you'll be liable for — particularly if the property is your own home, in which case the LMI is not tax-deductible. The second reason involves playing the banks at their own game — protecting yourself against any sudden downturn in the property market. Unnecessary exposure to market risk should be avoided at all costs.

Table 7.3: total loan size (including additionals) for a $500 000 property

Property's value (20% deposit = $100 000)	$500 000
Plus additionals:	
stamp duty	$22 000
legals (includes transfer and mortgage registration fee)	$3 000
adjustments	$2 000
Total additional costs	**$27 000**
Total loan size	**$400 000**
Deposit required	**$127 000**

Break fees on loans

Most banks in Australia charge clients purchasing a residential property a 'break fee' if the loan is to be repaid or refinanced within the first four years of inception. Each bank calculates these fees slightly differently, but the general charges incurred are calculated by:

◉ taking a percentage of the loan balance at the time of refinance or payout, calculated on a sliding scale. The longer you have had the loan, the less the fee will be

◉ charging a fixed amount. This fee is stated in the loan documents with an amount that will be charged at the time.

The break fees charged on a commercial loan are slightly higher than those charged on a standard residential home loan. Most commercial lenders will charge clients a break fee if they are to pay out the loan within the first three years of inception.

Unlike a residential loan, where you are charged a fee on the balance of the loan at the time of refinance or payout, commercial lenders charge a fee calculated by a percentage of the initial loan amount that was borrowed. Therefore this can be substantially higher as the initial loan amounts can be quite large.

A word on equity

Equity is the difference between the value of the property and the amount you owe on the loan. History shows us that a property purchased in the right area in close proximity to a capital city, with all available amenities, is more than likely to double in value every seven to 10 years.

Bear in mind that between 1998 and 2008 we had one of the biggest property booms on record, so it's best to assume the growth we've seen will slow, which is why throughout this chapter, I use a highly conservative time frame of 10 to 15 years for future property prices to double. But even with a halving of the current growth rate, property still stacks up as an outstanding investment.

Let's take a look at an example. Say you decide to buy a property worth $500000. To help fund this purchase you borrow 80 per cent of the property's value ($400000). At this point, the equity in the property is $100000 (the difference between $500000 and $400000). Even if your home loan was interest-only—so for the next 15 years you serviced only the interest component of the loan (not the principal)— the equity in that property after 15 years, by which time the property had doubled in value to $1 million, has increased to $600000 (the difference between $1 million and $400000). Table 7.4 (overleaf) shows this example (property A), plus two others (properties B and C) to provide a comparison of their growth in equity over 15 years.

However, remember that the cost of ownership (and your ability to service the loan) is the key. If property is such a good investment, with prices set to double, why not just buy a $10 million mansion and set yourself up for life? The answer, of course, is that not many of us could afford the repayments.

If you're buying a rental property, the rental yield will contribute to the cost (that is, reduce the cost of ownership). If it's your own home, you'd be paying rent anyway, so factor that into the equation.

Table 7.4: equity growth, assuming conservative doubling of house prices within 15 years

Year 1	Value	Loan	Equity (%)	Equity ($)
Property A	$500000	$400000	20	$100000
Property B	$750000	$600000	20	$150000
Property C	$1000000	$800000	20	$200000

Year 15	Value	Loan	Equity (%)	Equity ($)
Property A	$1000000	$400000	60	$600000
Property B	$1500000	$600000	60	$900000
Property C	$2000000	$800000	60	$1200000

You can own two properties outright before you retire

When it comes to property, there's a goal that I believe every working Australian can achieve — particularly those of you reading this right now, who are already making positive changes to your financial mindset. I want you to aim to purchase not one, but *two* properties during your working life.

Now, I can hear the cynical among you saying, 'Why stop at two properties? Let's go for 27!' Well, using the strategies in this book the possibilities are limitless — I'm actually being conservative with my target of two properties, but 27 may be stretching things a little.

As I've mentioned, a property purchased in a good area generally doubles in value every 10 to 15 years. The average working life is about 45 years (from age 20 to 65). This means that if you've developed a saving mindset and a homeownership focus by age 25, you have 40 years to achieve the goal of owning two properties outright. But still, a 35 year old who makes a conscious decision to focus on his or her financial future can still achieve this goal. Even if you're undertaking this journey at 45, you still have *20 years* to realise your goal.

Although the underlying principles are the same, there are some distinct differences between purchasing your own home and an investment property. But your first priority should be to buy your own home; and as long as it's the right type of property and in a good area, you can use the increase in its value to help fund further investments or to form part of your retirement income.

Most people can't afford to buy their 'dream' home or family home as their first property investment—chances are you don't earn as much now as you will in future years, and/or you haven't had time to save the required deposit. A more likely scenario is that, like me, you'll buy a smaller, less expensive home as your first purchase and live there for a few years while paying down some of that loan. This first property is your springboard into the market—in time, you'll use your equity in that property to buy a second property, your dream home. Then the first property becomes an investment property that generates an ongoing income stream in the form of rent. *Noice.*

The way you structure that first property purchase is vital, particularly for tax purposes. The loan structure is especially critical if that first property eventually becomes an investment property. The Income Tax Assessment Act (ITAA) prohibits debt shifting—that is, converting non-tax-deductible debt into deductible debt. In Australia, the interest on a loan for your principal place of residence is not tax-deductible, but the interest on an investment property is tax-deductible. As a general rule, I recommend to my clients that the loan structure for that first property purchase includes an offset account. You then pay the minimum monthly repayments on the loan and contribute as much as you can into the offset account. Always get a professional to help you out here, at least with your first purchase.

Most loans extend over a 25-year period, but you should aim to pay it off faster (between 15 and 20 years). Some strategies to do this include making fortnightly, rather than monthly, contributions and paying off more than the bank asks. (These strategies are discussed further in chapter 8.)

A word about debt shifting

Debt shifting is a practice that catches out many Australians, causing them to pay unnecessary tax. So it's important that you structure your loans as tax-effectively as possible, particularly the purchase of that first property.

Debt shifting is the process of paying down a significant portion of the principal on the loan of that first property, then using the equity in the property (via a redraw facility) to finance the deposit on your next purchase (your dream home). There's nothing wrong with this process in theory, and the banks allow you to do it. The problem is the portion you've redrawn will not be a tax-deductible loan against your first property (now the investment property), as it was used to purchase your family home (because interest on your principal place of residence is not tax-deductible).

The solution is to use an interest-only loan with an offset facility. That way, rather than paying down the principal of the loan, you pay only the interest, and any additional savings are paid into the offset account (which is an account that offsets the interest earned against interest incurred). The accumulated savings in the offset account are then used as a deposit on your next purchase (dream home), and as the original loan stays the same, there is no debt shifting. This gives you a full tax-deduction on all the interest of the original loan when that property becomes an investment.

This complicated subject is best explained using an example. Let's say our friend Steve bought his first property for $450 000, borrowing 80 per cent of the property's value ($360 000) with a standard principal-and-interest loan. After seven years of hard work — using the principles of saving and reducing expenditure on wants, and by increasing his disposable income (through promotions and general wage increases) — Steve had paid down the principal of the loan to $240 000. He can draw an additional $120 000 (as the bank has previously authorised pre-approval to $360 000) to help fund the deposit of his next property, which will become his principal place of residence. His existing home now becomes his investment property.

Unfortunately, however, that $120 000 redrawn to fund the deposit will not be tax-deductible — only the $240 000 will. The $120 000 is used to fund his principal place of residence (home), so Steve misses out on a massive annual tax deduction of $9600 (the interest on $120 000 at 8 per cent).

Now, imagine Steve had heeded my advice that, if you're going to purchase a property that will eventually become an investment property later on, you should:

- take out an interest-only loan

- attach an offset account to the loan

- pay the minimum interest instalment amounts each period

- pay any additional funds that you can contribute towards this property into the offset account.

Armed with an interest-only loan and an offset account, Steve pays only the *minimum* amount required on the loan and puts the balance (what he would otherwise be paying on a principal-and-interest loan) into the offset account (plus any additional savings he can afford). This will eventually form the basis of the deposit on his second property (somewhere around year 10 for someone aged 35 now).

Any additional money in that offset account 'offsets' the size of the loan; therefore, rather than pay an additional $120 000 off the principal, Steve instead put it into the offset account, where interest is calculated on $360 000 *less* the amount in the offset account ($120 000), so he pays interest only on the difference: $240 000. He can then use the $120 000 in his offset account to form part of the deposit for his next property purchase. There's no debt shifting, because the loan has not increased; it has remained at $360 000 (he's taken the funds from the offset account). Thus, he enjoys the best part of an additional $10 000 tax deduction annually.

The 'how to' of buying two properties during your working life

Okay, you've heard the strategy—and loved it. It's time now to take a look at the nuts and bolts of how *anyone* (yes, I'm talking to YOU) can actually buy two properties before they retire.

Remember the assumptions. If you buy a good property in the right area, it should double every 10 to 15 years. And Steve has already made a first property purchase of $450 000. I've also assumed that Steve will save $20 000 a year by putting all pay rises and bonuses directly into the offset account, and will stick to a budget so he can reduce his expenditure. After 10 years, he will have saved enough for a 20 per cent deposit on a $1 million property.

Steve's family then moves into the second property, while the first property becomes an investment property (that is, it's rented out). The loan stays the same — interest-only (which is now tax-deductible) — and some of the interest costs are now met by the tenants. Steve's focus then is to pay off the family (second) home loan, as it is not tax-deductible. Using techniques from chapters 4 and 5, and some tips from the next chapter, he should aim to pay off his home loan in much less time (15 to 20 years) than the average loan period. By the time the second home is paid off — in 15 years — he has five years to pay off the investment property loan before he retires (at age 65), which has stayed at $360 000. This may sound like a short period of time, but the property is now worth $1.5 million — at a 4.5 per cent yield, the rent received is $67 500. And by year 30 this rent will have increased even further (as the yield percentage is kept in line with the value of the property). Steve should be able to achieve that five-year target with this rent added to his home loan repayments.

Therefore, at age 65, Steve will have an investment property valued at $1.8 million, generating a yield of 4.5 per cent (rent of $81 000 per annum), and a family (second) home valued at $2.6 million — both owned outright.

The $81 000 received each year in rent is a great start to Steve's retirement income. When adjusted for the value of the money in 25 years' time, it actually equates to $40 000 in today's dollars. Add to this any shares or superannuation, and Steve has a very comfortable retirement ahead of him. Steve's homeownership journey (using an interest-only loan) is shown in table 7.5.

Okay, so it's one thing for a guy earning $140 000 a year to afford to do this, but what about people on lower salaries? Well, let's take a look at how Sarah can achieve the same outcome.

She's a quick learner, Sarah. She's gone from having a huge debt to being aware of her spending habits. Her new savings focus, and awareness of the long-term financial security provided by homeownership, means she's saved a deposit and is now ready to take the plunge.

Table 7.5: Steve's homeownership journey

	Year						
	1	5	10	15	20	25	30
Steve's age	35	40	45	50	55	60	65
Value of first property	$450 000	$600 000	$750 000	$900 000	$1 200 000	$1 500 000	$1 800 000
Loan value (principal remaining)	$360 000 (80%)						**$0** (Paid off in five years)
Offset account total (plus savings)	$20 000	$100 000	$200 000 (Used as deposit on property 2)	$0			
Value of second property	—	—	$1 000 000	$1 300 000	$1 650 000	$2 000 000	$2 600 000
Loan value	—	—	$800 000	$600 000	$300 000	**$0** (Second loan paid off)	$0

On her current income of $40 000 per annum, and using all the savings strategies discussed in earlier chapters, she is able to save $200 per week after expenses—this equates to just over $10 000 annually. If this is put in a high-interest bank account earning good compounding interest, and with the odd pay rise along the way, Sarah will have saved $100 000 in seven years—enough for a deposit on a $500 000 property. Her first loan will then be for $400 000 (80 per cent of the property's price). Sarah's homeownership journey (using an interest-only loan) is shown in table 7.6. You can see that by year 22 she will be able to purchase a second property worth $1 million.

As mentioned, it's crucial that your home loans are structured correctly, particularly for tax effectiveness. And beware: having an offset account can be dangerous for some people. As you pay money regularly into the offset account, you can see the value of your funds increasing and it can be tempting to dip into that account for wants (particularly when you're on a strict savings plan). This can really lead you off the path from your financial goal, so only use an offset account if you're disciplined.

Jay's hot tip

It can be hard to overcome the huge temptation to dip into your savings— especially if you've got $100 000 sitting in your offset account. Here are some ways you can avoid the lure of a new car or holiday:

- ○ Keep your eye on the prize. Always remind yourself of your goal: owning two properties.

- ○ Holidays should be paid with savings over and above your contributions to your offset account.

- ○ You'll get a bigger buzz out of being able to buy your dream home than the short-term buzz of frivolous purchases.

Table 7.6: Sarah's homeownership journey

	Year								
	1	7	12	17	22	27	32	37	42
Sarah's age	23	30	35	40	45	50	55	60	65
Value of first property	–	$500000	$650000	$800000	$1000000	$1300000	$1600000	$2000000	$2400000
Loan value (principal remaining)	–			$400000 (80%)					$0 (Paid off in five years)
Offset account total (plus savings)	$10000	$100000 (Used as deposit on property 1)	$60000	$120000	$200000 (Used as deposit on property 2)		$0		
Value of second property			–		$1000000	$1300000	$1600000	$2000000	$2400000
Loan value			–		$800000	$600000	$300000	$0 (Second loan paid off)	

Jay's take aways

- There are six things to do before buying a property:
  - conduct market research
  - save for a deposit, factoring in additionals—your deposit needs to account for 20 per cent of the purchase price plus additional costs, otherwise you'll be charged LMI
  - know how much you can borrow—before auction day
  - understand which type of loan is right for you
  - understand ownership structure
  - read (and understand) the fine print of your loan.
- Banks use the level of exposure (risk) and your ability to pay back the loan (serviceability) to assess your loan worthiness.
- Use principal-and-interest loans for purchases of a principal place of residence and interest-only loans with an offset account for investment properties.
- Equity is the difference between the value of the property and the amount you owe on the loan.
- A property purchased in the right area is likely to double in value every 10 to 15 years.
- You can buy two properties outright during your working life. Your first property (a small, less expensive home) is your springboard into the market. You can use the increase in its value to buy a second property, your dream home. The first property then becomes an investment property that generates an ongoing income stream in the form of rent.
- The structure of that first property purchase is vital, particularly for tax purposes—especially if that property eventually becomes an investment property (to avoid debt shifting).
- The interest on a loan for your principal place of residence is not tax-deductible, but the interest on an investment property is tax-deductible.

- Use an interest-only loan with an offset facility for your first purchase — any additional savings in the offset account form the deposit on your next purchase.

- Aim to pay off your home loan in 15 to 20 years.

- Beware the danger of an offset account.

Chapter 8

Beating the banks — strategies for mastering your home loan

What you'll discover in this chapter:

- ŏ the relationship between the US subprime fiasco and interest rates in Australia
- ŏ that you don't have to be loyal to your bank
- ŏ the benefits of using a mortgage broker
- ŏ how to work out the true rate of a home loan
- ŏ how repaying your loan fortnightly can save you interest.

Banks are a lot like boyfriends, girlfriends, husbands and wives — you can't live with 'em, you can't live without 'em. They're a necessary evil for anyone who wants to use leverage to fast-track the achievement of their financial goals.

Investors — from ordinary mums and dads to the big players — are worried about interest rates. Will they continue to rise, or perhaps slow down? One thing's for sure: between 2006 and 2008 interest rates rose dramatically — over two full percentage basis points.

Along with interest rates, the subprime mortgage crisis in the United States has dominated financial discussions. These issues are definitely linked and are a cause for concern for the average punter who is being bombarded with a seemingly constant stream of doom and gloom stories. One minute we're in an economic boom and have never had it so good, the next minute the sky's falling in … you'd be within your rights to ask: 'Did I miss a meeting?'

So, how did these issues arise and how are they related?

The US subprime crisis

The US subprime situation arose as a result of several financial institutions being overly generous with their lending arrangements for homebuyers. 'Subprime' refers to a type of loan where there are reduced loan-assessment requirements, meaning customers who might not otherwise have been able to obtain a loan could receive finance. This fuelled an already growing housing market, and thus many buyers felt emboldened to aim high and spend big. But there was a catch. Although the interest rates on subprime loans were often as low as 1 per cent or 2 per cent for the first two to three years of the loan, after this period the rates became significantly higher, catching many borrowers unawares.

Many subprime mortgagees took on their loans with the anticipation of refinancing at more favourable rates in the future (due to an expectation that house prices would continue to rise). However, once the overpriced US housing market began to flatten out, many subprime mortgagees were saddled with repayments that were unsustainable. Rather than default, most tried to sell their asset, further driving prices downwards. Confidence in the housing sector plummeted, and those in trouble now found it harder to sell their asset, resulting in large-scale defaults.

As the problem grew, larger institutions that had provided funds to the mortgage lenders became embroiled in the situation, having to write off millions (and sometimes billions) of dollars worth of loans. Companies that owned shares in these subprime institutions also took massive hits in their stock market value.

With all these bad debts (defaults), anyone lending money soon became nervous. Suddenly the good times, which had given lenders the confidence to lower their loan-assessment requirements further and further, were gone. As a consequence, the big end of town (lending institutions) raised the price of lending in order to cover present and future bad debts. This increase was passed on down the line, rippling all the way around the world to Australia.

Interest rates on the rise

From 2006 to 2008, interest rates have generally been on the rise. More recently, we've seen the first reduction in rates in over seven years. It's likely that rates will continue to fall into mid 2009.

Why the rise in interest rates? The Reserve Bank of Australia (RBA) was spooked by the possibility of inflation, which basically means a rise in the general price of goods over time. The RBA believed the economy was too strong, and a strong economy would lead to the dreaded inflation—which is an economist's version of the bogey man, Dracula and a dentist all rolled into one.

To slow down the economy, the RBA tried to curb spending by making credit harder to obtain (by increasing the 'cost' of money). It did this by raising the official cash rate, which affects you and me in the form of higher costs for all lending (felt most acutely by homeowners). The aim of these rises was to get consumers to spend less.

As figure 8.1 (overleaf) illustrates, we've never had it so good. According to the Australian Bureau of Statistics, between 1996 and 1997, and 2006 and 2007, real net national disposable income per person grew by 2.9 per cent a year on average, reaching $39000 in 2006–07. Australia's real net worth rose at an average rate of 0.9 per cent per year between June 1997 and June 2007, reaching over $254000 per person in 2007.

Yet now, like never before, home loan affordability is at an all-time low. Australians are spending more and more of their net disposable income on their mortgage repayments—and also their rent payments. At the time of writing, the average loan size is $330805 and the average deposit size for first-home buyers is about 10 per cent.

Nine ways to beat the banks (and none involves a balaclava)

What's a homebuyer to do? Well, let's take a look at some strategies to help you beat the banks at their own game, or at least give you some tools to ensure you get the best deal possible when seeking finance.

Figure 8.1: real net national disposable income per person

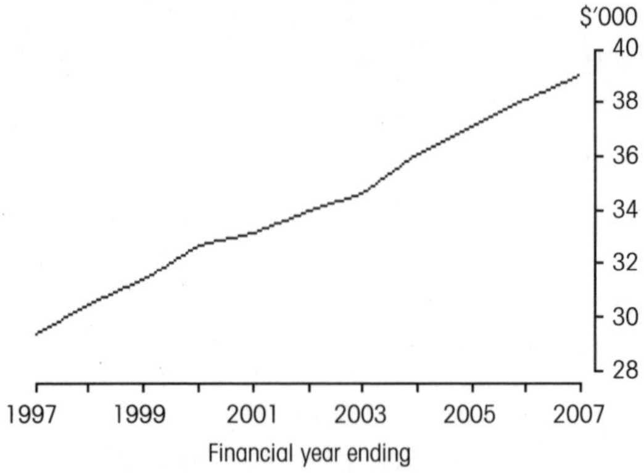

Source: 'Australian System of National Accounts' 2006–07, Cat. No. 5204.0. ABS data used with permission from the Australian Bureau of Statistics <www.abs.gov.au>.

Loyalty schmoyalty

Many Australians have an inherent loyalty in our DNA. It flows through to everything we do. We're loyal to our sporting teams, supporting them in good times and bad. We often stay in jobs longer than we should because we feel loyal to our employer, despite the fact that the boss is not as loyal to us as we'd like to believe (but of course if *my* team are reading this—which they'd *better* be if they want to keep working with me—I love you like my own offspring).

This same loyalty holds true with the banks. Most people probably bank with the same institution that they opened a kids' savings plan with while at school, or perhaps they bank where their parents have a home loan.

There's a pretty sound historical reason for loyalty to banks. Lending practices were stricter back in our parents' day. Banks were more reluctant to lend and you had to give them good cause why they should lend to you. Basically, you had to suck up big time. But that was then, this is now …

I don't recommend that you show the banks loyalty purely for the sake of it. Banks offer different products and not everyone has the right product for you. Sometimes you'll have to shop around to find the bank that's right for your particular circumstances.

Use a mortgage broker

There are 50-odd lenders in today's marketplace, ranging from the big four (Commonwealth Bank, ANZ, National Australia Bank and Westpac) to smaller, non-traditional lenders (building societies and credit unions), each with myriad products to choose from. It's often these smaller lenders that have the right products for our needs. Thankfully, there's a product to suit everyone — but it can be overwhelming. You have to do a lot of research to ensure you choose the right one.

When evaluating products, bear in mind that the banks often compete against each other for market share at different times during the year. For example, one bank may offer a 'professional pack' in March that is far better than any of its competitors (to gain market share among professionals in the residential sector). Then in May, another bank will offer a great deal for commercial products in order to get the jump on the competition.

If you don't have the time to research all the lenders and wade through the various products on offer, I recommend using a mortgage broker to help you find the right product for your needs. They will get an understanding of what your criteria are, then sift through the various lending options available to you and evaluate all available products to put together an appropriate strategy that meets your goals.

Generally, there's no up-front broker fee. The broker is paid by the lending institution through a commission on the business placed with them. The key is to source a reputable broker. Don't just go for someone who argues that he or she will get you the best rate — the best rate may not necessarily provide the right product for your particular circumstances. For example, without you realising, a mortgage broker may cross-collateralise two properties for the one loan, essentially meaning that both properties are used as security over the one loan, which may not be the right strategy for you in the future. The last thing you want is to focus all your energy on paying down a loan, only to realise the property is still encumbered with another loan.

Negotiate a better rate

If you decide to use a broker, *you* should be in control of the relationship. Explain to the broker what it is that you're after. It pays to do your research, so you know what you're talking about and you're better prepared when discussing options with the broker.

For example, most banks offer consumers a discount of up to 0.7 per cent for what they refer to as a professional package, so they've got room to bargain. The first thing you should ask your broker for is a 0.7 per cent discount off your product. Don't just go with what they tell you. Walk in there with the expectation that you'll get a discount off the standard variable rate. One thing's for sure—you won't get it if you don't ask!

Keep an eye on the fees

One of the ways banks compete against each other is to advertise a lower interest rate, but in actual fact have higher hidden fees, including application fees, transaction fees, internet fees, chequebook fees, split fees and exit fees … what next, breathing fees?

When comparing products, it's crucial to look beyond the advertised interest rate—you also need to address the associated fees for that loan. Use the fees and interest rate to calculate the associated costs to you each year in repaying that loan to determine the true rate. This is one of the value-added services a broker should provide.

Comparing products: the true rate

The Annualised Average Percentage Rate (AAPR), also called the true rate, helps you compare the total cost of a product—not just the advertised interest rate. It factors in all costs, including 'hidden' costs, to give you a better idea of the true cost of a loan. The AAPR also helps you see through the attraction of a 'honeymoon' rate, where year one has a low interest rate (the honeymoon), followed by several years of 'hangover'. The true interest rate is based on assumptions, so it's always best to get your broker or mortgage provider to compare products for you.

Let's compare two loans to find out their true rate. This example is based on a loan amount of \$300 000 over a 30-year term with two of a large bank's available products. Loan 1 is for a three-year fixed rate at 8.54 per cent, which then reverts to the standard variable rate of 9.33 per cent. Loan 2 is based on a product that provides a discount of 0.70 per cent through the life of the loan but has higher ongoing fees. This is shown in figure 8.2.

Figure 8.2: true rate and total cost of two loans

Loan details	Loan 1	Loan 2
Loan amount	$300000	$300000
Years	30	30
Fixed or intro. term in months	36	0
Fixed or intro. rate	8.54%	8.63%
Standard rate	9.33%	8.63%
Fees		
Application fee	$700	$100
Monthly fee	0	0
Annual fee	$96	$350
Discharge/exit fees	$300	$300
Total fees	$3880	$10900
Loan summary		
Intro monthly repayment	$2315	$2334
Ongoing repayments	$2477	$2334
Real interest rate	**9.17%**	**8.78%**
Interest paid	$585776	$540397
Total cost	**$889656**	**$851297**

As you can see, after considering all the other 'hidden costs', loan 2 with a true rate of 8.78 per cent is actually cheaper than loan 1 with a true rate of 9.17 per cent. Things aren't always what they seem!

Use an offset account

Nine times out of 10, I recommend that savvy investors consider offsetting any savings they've got in a mortgage offset account, which is a separate savings account linked to their home loan. Some banks refer to an offset account differently; for example, Commonwealth Bank refers to it as a Mortgage Interest Saver Account (MISA).

As mentioned in chapter 7, there are many advantages to an offset account. For a start, putting money into an offset account helps you dramatically reduce the amount of interest you're going to pay on the home loan. The balance of the offset account is offset daily against the loan amount. 'Notional' interest is earned at the same interest rate as your linked loan; this interest is offset against the interest payable on the loan.

If the loan is for your principal place of residence, and you're also looking to save money (say, for a deposit on another property), those savings should go into the offset account rather than into a separate bank account. As the loan is for your principal place of residence, it is not tax deductible. Also, if you had money in another account you'd have to pay tax on the interest earned. So by using an offset account, you have a double win.

An offset account can also help you avoid debt shifting. If the property is going to be your stepping stone to future property purchases, you can use the funds in the offset account as the deposit for your next property.

Pay off the home loan fortnightly (or even weekly)

Standard home loan repayments are due monthly. By sheer coincidence, monthly repayments happen to generate more interest revenue for the banks. Through the simple mathematics of compound interest, you'll find that repaying your loan fortnightly—or better still, weekly—can save you a dramatic amount of interest over the life of the loan.

On an average loan of $350000 with a typical interest rate of 8.70 per cent per annum the banks will request their customers pay a minimum monthly repayment of $2740.96 towards the loan over its lifetime. By dividing this repayment in half and making fortnightly repayments (of

$1370), the average consumers can save over $195 000 in interest and pay off the loan almost eight years earlier!

Why is this so? Well, the banks calculate the interest payable daily, therefore, the more often you make a repayment, the smaller the loan size on which the interest is calculated. However, if you were to ask to make fortnightly repayments when you first take out the loan, the actual repayment per fortnight would be less than $1370 (it would be $1265) so it would still take 30 years to repay the loan, and the bank would receive a similar amount in interest. So, calculate the monthly repayment amount for your loan, then halve it and pay it fortnightly—you stand to make huge savings! This can be seen in table 8.1.

Table 8.1: difference between monthly and fortnightly repayments on an average loan.

Repayment cycle	Amount	Total interest payable on loan	Saving on interest
Monthly	$2740.96	$636 749	$0
Fortnightly	$1370.48	$440 958	$195 791

Do your own research. Visit some of the many online mortgage calculators and compare the effect of changing your repayment period. These calculators can be found on any of the banks' websites and at <www.wheresmymoney.com.au>.

Consider an interest-only loan

You'll remember from the previous chapter that an interest-only (IO) loan, with an attached offset account, is a great way for savvy investors purchasing a first property to accelerate a move into their next property. By making the minimum interest repayments on the loan and maximising your contributions into the offset account, you can build up your savings over time and wind up with a substantial deposit that can then be used to acquire the next property.

There is a risk with this strategy, however. If you're a 'peacock' or a 'kookaburra', be careful not to access the offset account for wants, otherwise you'll never pay off the loan.

A principal-and-interest loan is a safer bet for anyone without the willpower to avoid dipping into the offset account. The downside is it'll take longer to achieve your financial goals—paying off the principal as you go chews into your income.

Refinance to pay off bad debt

If you're a disciplined investor with other 'bad' debt, such as personal loans or credit cards, and with equity in your property, I recommend you refinance that debt to a much cheaper interest rate. At the time of writing, the standard variable interest rate was 8.57 per cent (visit <www.wheresmymoney.com.au> for the latest rate), while interest charged on credit card debt is about 20 per cent. It makes sense, therefore, to refinance that debt using the equity in your property. Use the bank's money to pay out the credit card and put a disciplined system in place to ensure that your credit card debt is managed correctly.

Regularly review your circumstances

Three months is a long time in the finance game, let alone three years, so I strongly recommend a regular home loan review (every two to three years). The product you took out two years ago may be outdated, so quiz your broker regularly to ensure you have the right loan structure for your current situation.

Jay's take aways

- There's no value in being loyal to a bank for no reason—always be on the lookout for a better deal.
- Use a mortgage broker to help ensure you get the best product possible.
- Negotiate a better rate—the banks have a buffer to play with, so use it!
- Ensure you understand the fee structure of products, and be sure to compare apples with apples.
- If you can avoid dipping into them, offset accounts are a fantastic tool.

- Pay off your home loan fortnightly (or even weekly)—not monthly.

- Consider an interest-only loan, in conjunction with an offset account.

- Refinance to pay off bad (non-deductible) debt.

- Have a regular home loan check-up to make sure your existing product is still the best one for you.

Chapter 9

Share and share alike

What you'll discover in this chapter:

- shares are a vital part of a balanced, diversified investment portfolio
- with a long-term time frame, the rewards are worth the risks
- the difference between trading and investing
- the pros and cons of investing in the sharemarket versus investing in property
- the pros and cons of borrowing to buy shares.

For many people, the sharemarket conjures up images of rich guys in suits worth more than the average yearly salary, lounging on Chesterfields, smoking cigars and gazing over a floor-full of guys screaming, waving bits of paper and making indecipherable hand signals.

Yes, investing in the sharemarket—up against the 'big boys'—can be a daunting experience for the trading novice. Where do you start? How do you do it? How much do you need? And how does it all work?

The first thing I want you to understand is that the sharemarket is *not* just for the rich. It is a great investment opportunity for anyone reading this book, particularly when used in conjunction with other options, such as property, as part of an overall wealth creation strategy.

This book is not meant to be an A to Z of share investing, but this chapter will give you a basic understanding of how the sharemarket works—so that you feel confident enough to get involved—because every balanced investment plan should include shares. (Definitions of some common sharemarket terms and phrases are included in the glossary.) In fact, investing in shares is the seventh step on your journey to financial prosperity. So come with me, as I lift the veil of secrecy surrounding the sharemarket, and have a poke around so you feel ready to start investing. (But if you break anything, you buy it.)

What is the sharemarket?

Oooh, the big scary sharemarket … gimme a break. The sharemarket is just a trumped-up produce market—a group of buyers and sellers bidding and making offers on certain goods. But instead of trading fruit and vegetables, the sharemarket trades stakes (called stocks or shares) in the ownership of companies. When you purchase a stock, you're buying part-ownership of that company. There are other differences between produce markets and the sharemarket: usually you don't know who you're buying the stock from or who you're selling it to (unless it's an off-market transaction), and you require a broker (either a full-service or discount broker) to help you complete the transaction. But the principle is the same. They even have loud guys shouting stuff! [Er, Jay, those guys on the exchange floor went out with the internet. Get with the times, my man!]

Investing versus trading

There's a big difference between investing in the sharemarket and trading the market. Investing is a long-term wealth creation strategy, whereas trading is focused on short-term profits. Technically, everyone with superannuation is a sharemarket investor as this is primarily where super funds invest our future nest egg. With trading, you operate in a business-like manner, generally using technical or fundamental analysis (or a combination of both) to determine when to enter and exit the market, with a view to make a profit (yes, investing also aims to make a profit, but through growth over time rather than short-term fluctuations in share prices).

Trading is not a topic that I'll be concentrating on in this book—I'll leave that to experts like Louise Bedford and Chris Tate, who are both great friends and loyal clients of mine. (Visit their website <www.tradinggame.com.au> to pick up some terrific free information on how to trade effectively.)

Chris Tate is a trading veteran of 30 years and one of the first people to release a share trading book in Australia. He has had an extraordinary impact on thousands of traders. The best-selling author of *The Art of Trading* and *The Art of Options Trading in Australia*, his brutally honest approach and meticulous pursuit of excellence qualifies him as Australia's foremost derivatives trading expert.

I asked Chris to provide a few words of wisdom, should you decide to become a trader. His advice is:

> Trading effectively revolves around three specific rules:
>
> 1   If it's going up, buy it.
>
> 2   If it's going down, sell it.
>
> 3   Keep your position sizes small.
>
> After decades of trading, these are the basic rules that govern every trade that I make. Get these right and the rewards you can make from the sharemarket can be immense. However, you should be cautioned—you will never master the market. You will merely be fortunate enough to go in the direction it is going and to capitalise on this. In time, you may generate enough wisdom to realise what your appropriate responses should be. Develop a trading plan that covers your entry, exit and position sizing rules, and stick to it. No plan, no profit—it is that simple.

Louise Bedford has been a sharetrader for nearly 20 years and is Australia's best-selling sharemarket author. Her trading books—*Trading Secrets, Charting Secrets, The Secret of Candlestick Charting* and *The Secret of Writing Options*—as well as her presentations, are not about vague concepts that don't work in the real world. They are about incredibly practical, time-saving strategies that you need to implement in order to become an extremely successful trader. She states:

> If you can learn to accurately diagnose the trend of a share, and you have developed a written trading plan, the most essential area to consider is your own psychology. Your bank balance will rarely exceed your level of self-development, so you must work as hard on yourself as you do on your trading plan. Money is made as a

by-product of following a sound trading plan, yet to follow your plan takes guts, persistence and determination.

Investing, on the other hand, is something that we can all get involved in. I'm passionate about investing; so much so that I spent the time, money and effort a few years ago to become a qualified financial planner. I now spend just as much time on my clients' financial planning requirements as I do on their accounting needs.

Share investing versus property investing

Investing in the stock market is similar to property investment in many ways. Generally, our two main reasons for investing in property are to receive income (in the form of rent) and to benefit from the asset's appreciation in value. Other reasons include taking advantage of the negative gearing benefits that are offered with investment-property ownership.

Similarly, investing in shares also provides an income (in the form of dividends) and you benefit from asset-value appreciation (in the form of the share price increasing over time). Like property, the investment can also be negatively geared through processes called margin lending or instalment gearing, which we will look at shortly.

So why, after having read about how great property is as an investment, would you bother investing in the sharemarket? Well, let's look at some of the advantages and disadvantages of owning shares instead of property.

Why shares rock compared to property

Share investing has a number of advantages:

- The sharemarket is easier and less costly to get into and out of than the property market. To begin with, the entry and exit costs when buying and selling shares are significantly cheaper. Brokerage can be as little as $100 for a full-service broker and $20 for an online or discount broker. Compare that with the entry costs for property such as stamp duty (which can be as high as $25 000 on a $500 000 purchase) and exit fees (real estate agent fees can be anywhere from 1.5 to 2 per cent of the sale price).

- Shares are more liquid than property—meaning it's quicker and easier to get your money out of the sharemarket compared to the property market. When buying or selling shares, there's a three-day settlement period—referred to as T+3, meaning trade plus three. For example, if you bought shares on a Monday, you are required to settle (pay the full amount) by Thursday. If you sold on a Monday, you receive the proceeds of that sale on the Thursday. (This, of course, assumes the shares are available to buy or there are buyers when you want to sell. If you stick to the top 200, market liquidity is unlikely to be a problem.)

  Property is a completely different kettle of fish. You need to allow at least 30 days before you make the sale: getting the property ready to sell, engaging a real estate agent, advertising the property and holding open-for-inspections. Once you manage to sell, settlement can take anywhere from 30 to 180 days. The earliest you would be able to get your money is about 60 days.

- The sharemarket enables diversification. All robust investment portfolios should be diversified, so your risk is spread (it's that old saying, 'don't put all your eggs in one basket'). The sharemarket lets you diversify in two ways. Firstly, your investment portfolio is diversified away from property. Secondly, you can diversify within the sharemarket. There are various types of industries and indexes you can invest in—resources, health, biotech, banks, telcos, media, you name it. Quite often one sector can be 'up' (its stock values are rising), while others are down (in early 2008, the banks copped a hammering while resources stocks were well up on the back of the China-driven resources boom). As a general rule, however, when property's down, it's down across the board.

- In most cases, when we receive income from shares (in the form of dividends), tax has already been paid on those dividends, particularly for Australian shares—these are often referred to as franked dividends. (This doesn't mean the dividends were once owned by a guy called Frank.) You receive an imputation credit with franked dividends, which tells you that company tax has already been paid by the entity for the financial year, so you may not be liable to pay additional tax.

To illustrate, let's assume a company made a $100 million profit, on which it has paid company tax (30¢ in the dollar), so it has $70 million available to pay to shareholders, which it decides to do via dividends (the company could instead choose to reinvest some or all of its profits). Shareholders receive a net (after-tax) amount in dividends, but on their statement will be a gross (pre-tax) amount, which will account for the company tax that has already been paid. So dividends have generally had tax paid, whereas you will still need to pay tax on rental income.

- Shares don't require repairs and maintenance, there's no risk of fire or damage, and no concerns about vacancy. You're investing in a business; it's the job of the people who run it to take care of the 'repairs and maintenance' requirements for your investment. (And shares don't have tenants throwing wild parties—that you're never invited to.)

Why shares bite compared to property

It's not all rosy, though—there are some disadvantages to investing in shares instead of property.

- You can't live in your share portfolio (although you can make a great cubbyhouse from all your prospectuses). Although I counsel against it, it's comforting to know that if your world comes crashing down, you can always move into your investment property.

- The sharemarket is significantly more volatile than the property market—it's prone to sudden rises and falls. And there's a lot less warning about when there's going to be a crash than you usually get with property.

- When the stock market crashes, it's more dramatic. In 2008 we saw 4 and 5 per cent wiped off the stock market in a day. This is very rare in the property market.

- You can't get as much leverage on your investment. Banks will only lend around 70 per cent of a share portfolio containing good, strong blue-chip stocks (less for non–blue-chip shares). But with property, banks are prepared to lend more (up to 105 per cent of the property's value) because in their assessment the asset is more secure.

Another 'c' word

Okay, it's time to discuss another 'c' word—one that terrifies most would-be sharemarket investors (and plenty of current ones, too). It represents one of the biggest reasons holding people back from entering the market: crash. Just the sound of it is unsettling. Throw in words like recession and depression, and you can appreciate why many investors stick to seemingly safe bricks and mortar.

So…are shares safe?

I'm often asked by clients and friends if investing in the stock market is a good idea. They regularly hear doom and gloom stories about sharemarket falls, here or in the US, which the media is quick to report—and which tentative investors are keenly listening out for. It's enough to weaken their confidence in the stock market, even in times when it's flying.

At the time of writing, the world was in the midst of a financial crisis due to the US-driven credit crunch, which had a dramatic impact on global sharemarkets.

But when it comes to investing, I always come back to one word: timing. (If you've been paying attention, you'll know I mean time in the market, not timing the market.) If you want advice on when to enter the market, speak to trading experts such as Louise and Chris. But for the average investor, it doesn't matter when you time your entry into the market—your focus is long-term investing, which is what this book is about. So rather than being short-sighted and focusing on the last three, six or even 12 months, let's put on our investor hats and take a long-term view. Figure 9.1 (overleaf), which shows the All Ordinaries Accumulation Index over 21 years (from January 1987 to January 2008), demonstrates this perfectly.

As you can see, it's a very healthy outlook when you look over time (but that's hardly going to sell papers).

The botton line is if you had invested $10000 in the All Ordinaries Accumulation Index in January 1987, by January 2008 that $10000 would have grown to over $80000.

Figure 9.1: All Ordinaries Accumulation Index, 1987 to 2008

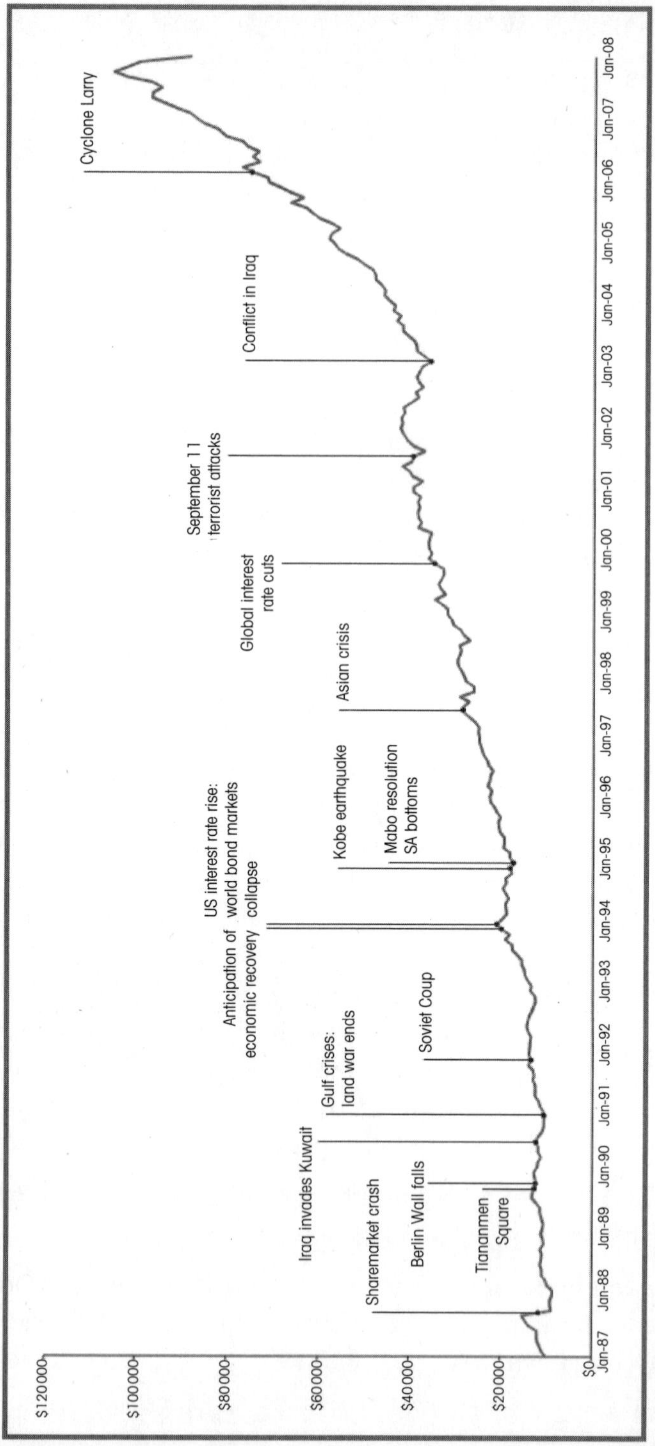

Source: IRESS, S&P, ASX.

Consider that during this period there have been terrorist attacks on Western targets (September 11 and the Bali bombings), two gulf wars and the bursting of the technology bubble. Pretty powerful huh?

While many people retreat from the stock market during uncertain times, it's worth noting that some expert commentators do the opposite.

Warren Buffett, CEO of Berkshire Hathaway and arguably the world's greatest investor, has said:

> The time to buy is when everyone else is too fearful to do so...A simple rule dictates my buying: be fearful when others are greedy, and be greedy when others are fearful...and most certainly fear is now widespread, gripping even seasoned investors. To be sure, investors are right to be wary of highly leveraged entities or businesses in weak competitive positions. But fears regarding the long-term prosperity of the nation's many sound companies make no sense.[1]

It's worth noting the impact of other significant world events on our local sharemarket. Table 9.1 shows four dramatic world events (World War I, the Great Depression, World War II and the 1970s oil crisis) and the seven-year average return on the Australian sharemarket after those events. I've also included the value of $100 000 after seven years.

Table 9.1: effect on the Australian sharemarket following four world events

	Average seven-year return after event (%)	Value of $100 000 seven years after event
World War I	15.19	$269 094
The Great Depression	17.38	$307 014
World War II	11.55	$214 925
1970s oil crisis	22.15	$405 746

Source: Cambridge Financial Planning, 'The next 7 years', Market Update, 27 October 2008.

---

1 W Buffett, 'Bad news a boon for investors', *The Australian Financial Review*, 20 October 2008.

I'm not suggesting you go out and whack $100 000 on the market without doing some serious homework; what I'm trying to highlight is the fantastic buying opportunity that a falling market can represent. As Buffett suggested, we may be experiencing one of the greatest discount sales of our lifetime.

A safer, more strategic entry into the market would be to drip feed your investment in periodically—referred to as dollar cost averaging or instalment gearing (which we look at later in this chapter).

Jay's hot tip

Beware another type of investment risk on top of those discussed in chapter 2 (permanent loss of capital, fluctuating returns, and not achieving your goals): inflation risk. But rather than this risk arising from an action, inflation risk refers to the risk of doing nothing. In many instances, inflation can 'outperform' bank interest and other 'safe' investment options (like the under-the-mattress job), meaning you end up effectively losing money. It's a great reminder that sometimes, not doing anything is the worst course of action.

Stock valuation methods

There are many different ways to assess the value of a stock such as the income valuation or discounted cashflow method, the price–earnings valuation method and the Gordon growth model. While these methods are too complicated for the scope of this book, here's an overview of one of the more common methods: the Rule of 72.

The Rule of 72 is not so much a stock valuation method as an economic principle. It summarises the compounding effect of investing and is characterised by an equation. If an investment generates a return of 7.2 per cent per annum, and you reinvest that return back into the investment each year, the Rule of 72 states that your portfolio will double every 10 years. This rule is a great indicator of an investment's effectiveness.

To calculate the number of years it will take for an investment to double, simply divide 72 by the anticipated return on that investment.

For example, if you're expecting a 5 per cent return each year, then divide 72 by 5 to learn that it will take 14.5 years.

(Just writing about this sexy concept gets me so excited, I almost grabbed the paper, went to the shares page, found a yield above 7 per cent and called a discount broker to get on board.)

Other considerations when investing in the sharemarket

There are four things you must address before taking the plunge into the sharemarket:

- *Diversification.* Investing in the sharemarket ensures your investment portfolio isn't all tied up in property. And the sharemarket provides further diversification opportunities: you can invest in different sectors (for example, banks and resources) and different markets (via international shares; the Australian sharemarket makes up less than 2 per cent of the world index, so global diversification offers big opportunities).

- *Risk profile.* As we saw in chapter 2, everyone has a different investment risk profile. Your age, income and other factors will influence the level of risk you are prepared to take. If you're closer to retirement age, your level of risk aversion will be higher than someone who is 30 years old. You'd be less likely to invest in a high-risk–high-return investment, because your timing means you can't weather the storm.

- *Market sentiment.* This refers to the attitude of investors and traders across the board. It is characterised by the terms bull and bear market. Market sentiment describes the human element of this supposedly sophisticated endeavour: fear, greed, doubt, overconfidence. Even though a stock may be a great investment, negative market sentiment can lead others to panic and sell, thus driving prices down. In 2008, for example, market sentiment was against the banks. Despite record profits, most banks felt an investor backlash due to the credit crisis. Market sentiment explains most of the corrections that occur—and why there are still profits to be made even when the market is falling.

- *Role of discipline.* Discipline is vital when it comes to Tim Tams—and investments. Many times you will be tested, as there are lots of other things you could do with the cash. But it's important to hang tough and stick to your long-term investment strategy. When I first began investing in the sharemarket, my wife and I were looking to renovate our house. There was a lot of heat on me to sell the shares so we could finish off the house sooner. As tempting as it was, I'm glad I stuck to my guns because I would have been kicking myself—the portfolio has doubled since then. Score one to Jay! (Only 3427 to go ...)

Types of investors

Alright, so I've got you all juiced up about the sharemarket—now how do you get amongst it? And what do you do when you get in there? Let's look at your options, based on your situation and experience:

- *Beginner.* Your sharemarket entry options include instalment gearing and margin lending into managed funds, or simply putting money regularly into a managed fund.

- *Intermediate.* Your options include purchasing direct shares and separately managed accounts (SMAs).

- *Sophisticated.* You can use a combination of direct shares, SMAs and structured investments, and focus on timing your entry and exits.

Whichever group you belong to, you need to decide whether to manage the investment yourself or to seek professional advice. There are arguments for both. As investors grow more educated and sophisticated, they naturally tend to become more involved and look after their own investments. Personally, I believe there's always a place for an adviser, no matter how sophisticated you are. (I can hear you now: 'Wow, surprise, surprise. The financial planner recommends getting professional advice'. But I also get a regular check-up from a professional ... I'm just lucky that the professional work for me.) The truth is, I believe in paying for three things: good suits, good wine and good advice, so I always recommend seeking advice and assistance before you manage your own shares.

I'll look more specifically at the role of investment advisers in chapter 12, but I encourage even the sophisticated investors to have a review with a financial planner every year to ensure they're getting the most out of their investments (that should get me on the good table at the financial planners' ball…one near the back so I can sneak out early—my god they're boring!).

Beginner investors

I love this quote: 'The expert in anything was once a beginner'. I consider myself a sophisticated investor now, but I too began my sharemarket investing journey as a novice.

There are many types of strategies to get into the market. But for beginners (and even intermediate investors), I recommend an investment strategy called instalment gearing—also referred to as dollar cost averaging. You contribute regular (monthly) amounts of your own cash, matched (or doubled) by money you lend from the bank. It's like a savings plan for share acquisition. But the real key is using the power of leverage (borrowing) to fast-track your managed fund's growth.

You invest these contributions into a managed fund, which is a collection of various shares or investments that is managed by a fund manager (who specialises in putting share portfolios together).

Jay's hot tip

There are hundreds of managed funds you can choose from, ranging from conservative to aggressive. Your risk profile will dictate which managed fund is right for you. Therefore it's prudent that you sit down with a financial adviser to work out which one to choose. (See chapter 12 for tips on choosing a financial adviser.)

To start, you need somewhere between $1000 and $2000 as an initial investment into your managed fund. You then add to this with regular, consistent contributions of any amount—$250, $500, $1000—whatever you can afford.

Instalment gearing might be right for you if you:

- have a long-term goal

- are disciplined (you have the courage to stay in the market, even if it declines—which it will from time to time)

- are chasing a tax break (that is, you have a heartbeat)

- you want a strategy that works, even when the market is down.

Instalment gearing provides tax benefits similar to negative gearing an investment property. The interest you pay on the loan is tax-deductible, giving you a nice boost to your tax return at the end of the year. And like all good investors, you should reinvest that tax refund back into your investment.

It's not the only way to go, but if you want maximum bang for your buck, this is how you do it. I made my first foray into the sharemarket with instalment gearing, way back in 1997—and I still do it now. So I'm living proof it works.

Let's take a look at an example of how your instalment gearing plan will work. Say you kick-start your investment with $2000. Your instalment gearing can begin with a regular contribution of just $250 per month. With your $250 contribution, the bank will lend to you on a ratio between 1:1 ($250) and 1:2 ($500).

Borrowing 1:2 is pretty aggressive in today's climate (remember, you need to be aware of margin calls when borrowing for shares). So play it safe and borrow 1:1. This way you contribute $500 every month, of which $250 is yours and $250 is borrowed, so at the end of the year you've actually contributed $6000 plus your initial $2000 investment, totalling $8000. As mentioned earlier, the interest on the amount you have borrowed is generally tax-deductible. The interest rate is slightly higher than the rate you would pay for property due to the higher risk for the bank.

Every year, increase the amount you contribute (this will be funded by pay increases, and the other income-increasing methods outlined in chapter 5). Table 9.2 shows how your contributions could increase over time.

Table 9.2: increase of instalment gearing contributions over time

Year	Your monthly contribution	What you borrow each month
1	$250	$250
2	$300	$300
3	$500	$500

This is how I started investing in the sharemarket. I contributed $250 every month and borrowed $500 (which is a little more aggressive than I now recommend). As my income has increased, so have my contributions—I contribute $2000 every month and borrow $2500 each month.

Instalment gearing is a great way to build wealth, particularly if you reinvest the proceeds (dividends) back into the investment (using the Rule of 72). It's also a tax-effective investment strategy as the interest associated with the loan is tax-deductible. As a general rule, these loans are interest-only, and when you pay them off will be dictated by your wealth creation plan and/or your circumstances. This could go on until you retire, but it depends on your ability to service the interest each month. So your situation, and your plan, will dictate when and how you pay off the loan.

Margin lending

Margin lending is a little different. Rather than putting in regular contributions, you invest a lump sum amount and you gear (borrow) against that lump sum. You might start with a $10000 portfolio, borrow another $10000 (total $20000) and reinvest the dividends or trust distributions into that investment. This is a good strategy for people who have a lump sum to invest (such as equity in property) and want to accelerate their participation in the sharemarket.

A note on loans for shares

If you're considering leveraging (borrowing) to ramp up your entry into the sharemarket, you need to be aware that the sharemarket's volatility makes lenders more cautious. When borrowing to buy shares, lenders require a higher loan to value ratio (LVR) and will charge a higher interest rate than a loan for property.

The LVR determines the minimum amount of money you need to contribute, compared with the amount you borrow. For example, an LVR of 70 per cent means you must contribute 30 per cent of your own funds to purchase the security (the shares). Each margin lender has an approved securities list that can be used in a portfolio with each investment's LVR ranging somewhere between 40 per cent and 80 per cent. The LVR allocated to each approved security is under constant review from the loan provider resulting in regular LVR adjustments, depending on the security's performance and market-related conditions. For shares, a company has to meet minimum requirements to be approved. Typically, normal requirements include minimum market capitalisation of $100 million, demonstrated profit results and high liquidity.

From an investor's point of view, the LVR of the portfolio will constantly change due to the performance of the underlying investments (that is, the share price movements). If an investor's LVR reaches an unacceptable level, often around 80 per cent, the investor will receive a 'margin call', meaning he or she needs to repay the loan to bring the LVR back to the level required by the margin lender, normally 70 per cent. Repaying the loan can be done in two ways: the investor can use his or her own cash reserves, or sell some shares to repay the loan.

To clarify margin calls, let's take a look at an example, using the great Australian company, BHP Billiton.

In May 2008 Tom decided to invest $10000 in BHP shares, which were trading at $45 per share. Rather than use all of his own money he decided to margin lend. He used $3000 of his own money and borrowed the remaining $7000. He had 222 shares valued at $10000, with an LVR of 70 per cent.

Come September 2008, the loan was still at $7000 (as he was just servicing the interest, not the principal). However, the share price had fallen $10 to $35, which meant the shares were now worth $7770. This in turn meant that Tom's equity had fallen from $3000 to just $770. This drop in value pushed his LVR up to 90 per cent. This made the bank very nervous, so it issued Tom with a margin call, giving him two options to reinstate the LVR back to an acceptable level (70 per cent):

- He could sell some shares to fund the margin call (that is, he'll pay down the loan).

- He could tip in more money to move his LVR back under 70 per cent.

If Tom has the cash reserves to accommodate, and because BHP is a good investment, I'd recommend Tom take advantage of the fact that BHP is undervalued, and buy more.

(I found myself in exactly this scenario in April 2000. I received a margin call, and I wasn't happy. But in hindsight, it turned out to be a blessing in disguise. The margin call led me to buy more shares, which was great because the stock market was undervalued. This was of great benefit to my share portfolio in the long run.)

Of course, if Tom had kicked in more of his own money in the first place, and borrowed less, he would have had a safer LVR. If Tom put in $5000 himself and just borrowed $5000, he would have had the same share value ($10 000) and same share quantity (222), but a lower LVR (50 per cent). When the share price dropped from $45 to $35, his LVR would have dropped to 64 per cent—so he's not in margin call territory.

When should beginners get into the sharemarket?

Ideally, beginners should put this book down, pick up the phone and call a broker to get started in the sharemarket as soon as possible. (Then pick the book back up again because there are plenty more gems where this came from.) This may not fit with your investment strategy, however—for example, when you're saving for a deposit in the short term (say, three years) you don't have the time frame to ride out the ups and downs.

Another instance where the sharemarket may not be right for you just now is when your cash flow simply doesn't permit it. It's no use putting yourself under financial pressure just to try to leapfrog ahead; you gotta crawl before you can walk.

Let's use our case studies to take a look at some real-world scenarios.

In chapter 2, we saw that Sarah had a cautious risk profile. Her first priority was paying off her debts. Following that, she wanted to save for a deposit on a house. So my advice to her was that she wasn't ready for the sharemarket at that time.

Once Sarah pays off her debts, I would recommend she enter a seven-year plan to save for a deposit on a house. There are several ways she can do this: she can put her savings in a safe, secure (and low-earning) bank account, or she can be more aggressive and earn more in the sharemarket. For anyone with a shorter time frame, I wouldn't recommend the sharemarket as it can fluctuate. However, with a seven-year time frame, Sarah can afford to ride out any fluctuations, and history tells us she'll be well ahead of where she'd be had she put her savings in a bank account.

Table 9.3 compares the returns from Sarah's investment options over a seven-year period.

Table 9.3: comparison of returns over a seven-year period

Investment	Amount invested	Average return (%)	Total after seven years
Bank account	$800 per month	6	$83 000
Sharemarket	$800 per month	10.5 (6% growth, 4.5% income)	$97 500

Steve, however, already had a house; and, like most Australians, his investment portfolio was overweighted in property. Steve also had a spending problem and, consequently, a negative net disposable income. And as I mentioned earlier, one of the best ways to combat that is to take the temptation away from yourself. A great way to do this is to invest money you would otherwise spend on wants; say, by putting it in a managed fund. A high-income earner, Steve incurs a high tax rate. He can maximise his tax benefits through instalment gearing—effectively, he'd be negatively gearing a share portfolio. Steve also has the time frame to ride out any sharemarket fluctuations, so his risk profile is assertive/aggressive. I would encourage him to put any surplus net disposable income into the sharemarket.

Brad and Cindy's primary goal was to set up a business. Their secondary goal was to save for a deposit on a rental property within three years. All their disposable cash went towards the investment property deposit. Also, they didn't have the time frame to ride out any fluctuations in the stock market, so their risk profile was prudent, meaning they should play it safe in the short term and stick their money in a high-interest bank account.

Jay's hot tip

ô   Always invest in both property and shares if you can afford it.

ô   Avoid putting all your savings in the sharemarket if you've got a short-term focus (for example, less than five years) to get a house deposit.

Intermediate investors

Intermediate investors have a little more experience and investment nous, and usually more time and disposable income to be involved in their investments. They prefer to be more hands-on in choosing the stocks they invest in and/or their portfolio mix. Intermediate investors generally either use what's called a separately managed account (SMA) to buy direct shares, or a stock broker or financial planner to help them decide which direct shares to have in their share portfolio.

There are a number of strategies intermediate investors can use to help decide which direct shares to buy. These include:

- focusing on the top 20 yielders
- using the one-third, one-third, one-third method
- investing in SMAs.

Let's take a look at each.

Top 20 yielders

The 'top 20 yielders' is not a wrestling move—it's a common investment strategy that's been around for quite a while. The share price is the most commonly used signal of a share's value, but the top 20 yielders strategy focuses on the yield percentage rather than the share price. To calculate the yield percentage, divide the dividend paid by the share price. The essence of this strategy is that stocks with the highest yield are in actual fact undervalued.

To understand the concept of a stock's value, let's look at an example using something most people are more familiar with—property. Say you're looking to buy an investment property and you come across a $500 000 house that generates rent of $500 per week ($25 000 per year). The rental yield is 5 per cent ($25 000 divided by $500 000). The owner is desperate to sell, and you're able to pick it up for $250 000—so the house is obviously undervalued. You'll still receive the same dollar amount in rent, however, as the rental yield is a function of the cost, it has now doubled to 10 per cent—the yield percentage is much higher than normal.

It's the same with stocks—except you have a much greater chance of getting an undervalued stock than an undervalued house. Focus on the top 20 stocks on the Australian stock market by market capitalisation, as these are strong and stable stocks with high liquidity, and are traded every day. Of these 20 stocks, identify those with the highest yield percentage, then invest in the best four or five yielders. And keep reinvesting the dividends back into your portfolio.

Table 9.4 shows the top 20 companies on the ASX by market capitalisation as at 24 October 2008. (You can find the latest top 20 in newspapers, on the internet, or on the ASX website.)

One-third, one-third, one-third

The 'one-third, one-third, one-third' strategy ensures a good spread of asset classes to provide extra security (through diversity) while also allowing you to take advantage of high-performing classes. You simply divide your investment capital (for example, $100 000) across three classes: invest 33 per cent ($33 000) in direct cash, 33 per cent in Australian shares and 33 per cent in listed property trusts (like investing in property, but the property trusts are actually listed on the stock market; for example, Westfield Holdings).

Of course, you can ignore all this and go follow the latest market guru. (But there's far too much sitting cross-legged and incense-burning for me). My advice is to educate yourself and learn as many different techniques as possible, but stick to basic, sound professional advice—at least while you're starting out.

Table 9.4: top 20 companies on the ASX by market capitalisation (as at 24 October 2008)

ASX code	Company	Market capitalisation
BHP	BHP Billiton	$459744374
WDC	Westfield Group	$230477937
ANZ	ANZ Bank	$197683717
CBA	Commonwealth Bank	$173995511
WBC	Westpac Banking Corporation	$170809446
RIO	Rio Tinto	$164068407
NAB	National Australia Bank	$159655297
NCM	Newcrest Mining	$119849351
CSL	CSL	$87077100
TLS	Telstra Corporation	$86325811
STO	Santos	$66063070
WOW	Woolworths	$64824571
WES	Wesfarmers	$51260032
MQG	Macquarie Group	$48786947
WPL	Woodside Petroleum	$47446010
QBE	QBE Insurance Group	$43871063
ORG	Origin Energy	$42431536
SGP	Stockland	$41353692
SGB	St George Bank	$32861208
FMG	Fortescue Metals Group	$31445861

Separately managed accounts

Separately managed accounts (SMAs) are a new option for intermediate investors. An SMA is essentially a collection of shares inside a wrap account, similar to a managed fund. (A wrap account is an administration-type service that you can use to house your portfolio for ease of management and reporting.) The key difference is that with SMAs, you enjoy the benefit of actually owning the shares. Investing in SMAs is a great way for intermediate investors to directly own shares while maintaining diversity within their portfolio. Negative press on funds manager fees, and their lack of transparency, has seen SMAs grow in popularity.

The best way to start an investment in SMAs is to get your financial planner to help you determine your risk profile and subsequent asset allocation. He or she will determine the appropriate model portfolio for you and purchase the SMAs on your behalf.

Sophisticated investors

More astute investors who want a lot more involvement in their share activities are classed as sophisticated investors. These people are traders rather than investors, so I'll keep this brief as my focus is investing rather than trading. Sophisticated investors buy specific stocks for a specific reason and manage their risk by using facilities such as structured products (capital-protected investment portfolios generally over a period of five years). They also use international funds to spread their risk and minimise their exposure to just one market.

Jay's hot tip

In tough times such as the credit crunch, it's worth remembering that many experts make money when the market is falling rapidly (through techniques known as shorting) as there are bargains a-plenty to be had; so it's not *all* bad. Louise Bedford says:

There are lots of ways to make money out of a downtrend and in a volatile market. The first thing you should do is to exit any of your shares that have hit your stop loss. Then you can look to make a profit by using CFDs to short sell, or you could investigate options. You can write call options or buy put options and this can be incredibly lucrative. Once you've learned about these strategies, it's fairly simple to develop a twinkle in your eye any time the market has a correction, because you realise it will put money directly into your pocket!

For more information on these concepts, and for advice on how sophisticated investors can get started, visit <www.wheresmymoney. com.au>.

A final word on the sharemarket

By now you should be ready to embark on your sharemarket journey. Before you do, however, there are a couple of other things to consider.

Know yourself

I've focused on beginners, as you're the ones who need the most convincing about entering the sharemarket — intermediate and sophisticated investors will already be well aware of the benefits of investing in the sharemarket over a long time frame. Plus, intermediate and sophisticated investors already have some exposure to the market.

However, intermediate investors can still utilise the instalment gearing example provided in the beginners section, on top of any existing activities.

Sophisticated gurus should be speaking to experts such as Chris Tate and Louise Bedford to develop strategies and techniques to improve their returns in a safe manner.

Diversify

Sharemarket investing is an important way to diversify your investment portfolio and reduce your reliance on property investment. Yes, it's more volatile than other forms of investment, but higher returns only come with higher risk. Anyone looking to boost their investment returns (over the long term) should be in the sharemarket.

In times of market uncertainty, such as the recent US-driven credit crisis, dollar cost averaging and instalment gearing are great ways to invest. It's times like these when your funds manager can pick up some undervalued stocks. Indeed, a bear market (a declining market) is a fantastic opportunity for investors.

By now you've realised the benefits associated with investing in the sharemarket — not just the direct benefits discussed in this chapter, but also the indirect benefits — in particular the ability to diversify your asset allocation; particularly important, as the majority of Australians' investment portfolios are overweighted in property.

Therefore, if your risk profile permits, the time to get in the sharemarket is now.

Jay's take aways

- The sharemarket is an awesome way to diversify your investment portfolio and make cash in the long term (as part of an overall wealth creation strategy).

- Many people are scared off by the complexity of the sharemarket, but armed with some basic knowledge and the right advice, anyone can invest successfully.

- Sharemarket investing is a long-term wealth creation strategy, whereas trading focuses on short-term profits.

- Shares can be negatively geared through processes called margin lending or instalment gearing.

- Investing in the stock market is similar to property. You receive an income (in the form of dividends), benefit from asset value appreciation (in the form of the share price increasing over time) and enjoy the tax benefits of negative gearing.

  - Shares rock compared to property because of lower entry and exit costs, higher liquidity, diversification, and no worries about repairs, maintenance or damage.

  - Shares bite compared to property because of greater volatility — if disaster strikes, you can't live in your share portfolio; crashes are more dramatic; lenders require more security for shares (and will lend less); and you may receive margin calls.

- Crashes, recessions and depressions are a threat, but long-term investors can weather these storms — over time, the sharemarket is still a great investment despite these short-term threats.

- Use the compounding effect of investing: if you reinvest the returns from an investment generating a return of 7.2 per cent per annum, your portfolio will double every 10 years (the Rule of 72).

- Diversify your investment portfolio to spread your risk.

- Understanding your risk profile (how long you have in the market) will help guide your investment choices — but remember, there's even a risk in doing nothing!

- Market sentiment (characterised by the terms bull and bear market) explains most of the corrections that occur.

- Be disciplined. There are always lots of other things you could do with the cash, but you need to hang tough and stick to your long-term investment strategy.

- Beginners in the sharemarket can get started through instalment gearing and margin lending (or putting their own cash) into managed funds.

- Intermediate investors generally purchase direct shares (with the help of a stockbroker or financial planner) and separately managed accounts (SMAs).

- Sophisticated investors use a combination of direct shares, SMAs and structured investments, and focus on timing their entry and exit.

- Strategies to help determine which direct shares to own include the 'top 20 yielders' strategy and the 'one-third, one-third, one-third' strategy.

- Separately managed accounts (SMAs) are a collection of shares similar to a managed fund, but with the benefit of owning the shares.

- Strongly consider getting an adviser, no matter how sophisticated you are.

- Instalment gearing is a great way to build wealth, particularly if you reinvest the proceeds (dividends) back into the investment (using the Rule of 72). It's also a tax-effective investment strategy as the interest on the loan is tax deductible.

- Margin lending differs from instalment gearing because you invest a lump sum and gear against (lend) that same amount, rather than making regular contributions.

- $10 000 invested in June 1987 would be worth over $80 000 20 years later.

Chapter 10

Takin' care of business

> **What you'll discover in this chapter:**
>
> ☉ why owning a business is not for everyone
>
> ☉ focus on the four pillars of business: people, processes, customers and financials (in that order)
>
> ☉ the difference between being in business and being self-employed
>
> ☉ the biggest challenges facing business owners these days
>
> ☉ the four steps to a successful business.

As a business owner myself you may think I'm biased, but the simple fact is, owning a business is leverage in its ultimate state. If you really want to maximise your time, use someone else's! In fact, owning a business happens to be the eighth step on your wealth creation journey.

Rather than generating leverage from things such as property or shares, a business generates leverage from other people's time. When compared with a normal nine-to-five job where you generate an output of up to 40 hours a week, a business with 25 employees (like mine) produces 1000 hours a week—an outstanding return on your own eight hours per day. It's this opportunity that leads many people to invest most of their wealth in a business.

Not too long ago, I was considering purchasing a commercial premises for my business to avoid the burgeoning rent bill. But Mike Woolhouse,

CEO of boutique stockbroking firm Lodge Partners (and a client and good friend of mine), set me straight.

'Jay, my boy,' he began (Mike's a *lot* older than I am), 'why would you borrow $2 million for a measly 10 per cent return on a commercial property, when you could reinvest that money into your business and generate a return of between 30 and 40 per cent per annum? You'd be better off purchasing a similar type of accounting and financial planning practice'. I had to admit, he had me there. But I made sure he paid for lunch, so I think I broke even.

It's exactly this sort of thought process (or more correctly, the potential returns) that encourages many people to start their own business.

Owning a business is not for everyone

The traditional business model is not suited to everybody. There are a number of reasons for this:

- No matter how hard they try or how much they work at it, some people are not *people*-people—they don't have the ability to be leaders, let alone managers. And when running a business, which is all about using other people's time, you need to be a good leader or manager to get the most out of your people.

- The opportunity cost of leaving their current employment is too high for some people; therefore, the risk is too high. When my business partner and I started our business, we were 24 years old. I had a reasonable income for a bloke that age, earning around $50 000 a year at Ford, but, importantly, I had minimal expenses and no responsibilities. People currently earning between $100 000 and $150 000 with a massive mortgage and growing family obviously face much higher risks. These people could consider a transitional arrangement; for example, establishing a smaller business that can be run from home. The benefits of doing this include less financial risk, fewer and more family friendly hours, and the potential for both partners to be involved.

- Barriers to entry are quite high and can vary wildly. You may need a $30 000 working capital float for a professional services business (like my partner and I needed when we started our business). The average franchise will set you back $250000 upfront, while a trucking or transport business will set you back the cost of a truck.

Despite all this, there are various business options to consider while still maintaining your current place of employment.

Jay's hot tip

Here are five must-read books for anyone in—or thinking of investing in—a business:

- ð *Rich Dad, Poor Dad* and *The Cashflow Quadrant* by Robert Kiyosaki
- ð *The E-Myth Revisited* by Michael Gerber
- ð *The 4-Hour Workweek* by Timothy Ferriss
- ð *Show Mummy the Money* by Sonia Williams

How I got into business

My business story begins with my parents, predominantly my father. Like all young boys I idolised my dad, and, for as long as I can remember, he has always owned his own business—and was always in control of his own destiny. He began his career as a truck driver (owner-driver), doing various forms of haulage, from furniture removal to semi-trailers. From there he began a cane furniture importing business and today he runs a very successful industrial supplies business. But it wasn't always smooth sailing—and it was during these tough times that I learned the most about my dad's character and resolve.

For a number of reasons, the cane furniture business fell over, leaving my folks $100000 in debt—a huge sum of money back then (considering a house would only set you back $25000). And even though his business partner took off to Queensland, Mum and Dad honoured their financial commitments. They knuckled down to get back on an even footing. Dad worked three different jobs and Mum worked full time as well as being a full-time Mum. They sold the family home in Essendon and we moved into Nan's house in Pascoe Vale.

We pulled together as a family unit—Nan's house became a mini sweatshop, with a couple of different production lines on the go at any one time. After school the kids would help out on the latest project: anything from creating cosmetic jewellery to assembling household taps. We also did cleaning jobs. Eventually, we raised enough money to pay off all the debts and we were ready to start life over again. We moved out of Nan's house, and Mum and Dad went back into business.

The lessons I learned from this time still hold true to me today:

- Never, ever give up. Never concede defeat. Mum and Dad knew the hard yards they had to do to get to where they wanted to be. It was a case of 'head down, bum up' until the job was done.

- Businesses come in all shapes and sizes and can help you rise above adversity. Some people would look at my parents' debt as an insurmountable obstacle, but with five years of sacrifice and hard work undertaking a range of small business projects, they achieved their goal and enjoyed that sense of coming from behind to 'win'.

- Even if you've already attempted setting up a business and it didn't go to plan, this doesn't mean your second or third business won't succeed. My parents' example demonstrates that if at first you don't succeed, have another crack. Make changes by all means—adversity only becomes failure if we don't learn from it. Starting or owning a business isn't a walk in the park—if it was, everyone would be a business owner and there'd be no-one to actually work in the businesses!

The four pillars of business

All businesses have four key things in common, which I introduced in chapter 5. How well you develop these four aspects of your business dictates how successful it will be. The four pillars of business are:

- people
- processes
- customers
- financials.

Whether you're running an accounting and financial solutions practice, an industrial supplies business, cane furniture importing or building cars, you've got to work on these four areas of your business.

If you want to be successful, you'll need to master what's called the balanced scorecard reporting approach. This management tool reports on the four business pillars to give a holistic view of your performance. Rather than just report on your financials, you also report on your people, your processes and your customers.

For many small business owners, the first thing they do is prepare a budget. This is very important, but it is only one of the four components of the balanced scorecard (financials), and only a part of that component. In actual fact (and I'm gonna be cut from the accountants' ball for saying this), financials are the *last* thing you should be focusing on. Don't get me wrong, they're still an incredibly important component; it's just that your people need to come first—without them, there are no financials to concern yourself with (other than losses).

Let's look at each of the four pillars in turn, starting with the most important first.

People

Business is the ultimate form of leverage—getting leverage from other people's time. As such, you always need to remember that's what you're essentially dealing with: other people. Without them, you wouldn't have a business. If you didn't have any people in your business, you'd be self-employed. So if you want your business to be a success, put the time and energy into developing a great team.

A friend of mine, David Schwarz, former AFL player for Melbourne, has been a leader for many years now—originally on the football field as vice captain, now in business and the media. He strongly believes that 99 per cent of people genuinely want to do a good job and be seen as a valuable contributor. He likens it to the football field (like he does every bloody thing). If a player mucks up, he knows he's done wrong—the coach doesn't need to drag him. Likewise, it's no use the coach harassing him to do better. All the coach needs to do is provide a sound vision (game plan) and reinforce what is expected through training.

Similarly, the last thing people want is us managers leaning over their shoulder, asking, 'Have you done it yet? When will it be finished?' Rather, they want you to provide them with clear instructions on what your expectations are and let them run with it. They then get the buzz of coming to you with completed tasks and asking for the next one.

Michael Gerber, author of *The E-Myth* and *The E-Myth Revisited*, asks, 'Can you actually motivate people?' He suggests you can't. You can inspire them, but motivation comes from within. It's something to consider, especially with all the motivational speakers out there. As leaders, owners and shareholders, our role is not to 'motivate' people solely through carrots (bonuses) or sticks (cracking the whip); rather, we should inspire them, lead by example and let them develop their own motivation.

You gotta know when to hold 'em

One of the biggest challenges most businesses face today (including mine) is attracting and retaining key team members. We adapted our vision to turn this negative into an opportunity. Rather than work hard to find great team members, we created a culture that engages our team members to help find new members.

We asked ourselves what we wanted our people to look like in three years' time. Once we got rid of the joker who kept saying 'Charlize Theron', we agreed we wanted them to be:

- *proud to be part of a high-performance team*. We wanted an integrated team that worked together with integrity to help our clients achieve their overall objectives

- *problem solvers*. They should be focused on continual professional development, so that our business would be seen as a talent magnet — people would want to come and work at The Practice

- *referrers*. We wanted our people to want to work with like-minded people so they would help us recruit and attract guns to our organisation.

At The Practice, we created a bonus or incentive scheme that linked individual targets to the overall objectives of the firm. The system was designed to promote teamwork and cross-referrals between the different departments. We also developed a tailored training program focused on continual professional development (CPD) for every team member to ensure everyone could achieve their CPD hour requirement, as required by all professionals (30 to 40 hours per year). The other benefit was that the firm as a whole was 'skilled up' in all areas. In addition, we nominated one of our future leaders to be director of training. Finally, we developed a system that provided an incentive for our team members to recruit for the firm—they get paid a spotters fee for introducing a new employee. Team members are also encouraged to attend fairs and university open days to source the best up-and-coming talent.

Has this approach worked for us? The proof is in the pudding. We now have 25 like-minded team members in our organisation who have come from a variety of sources, including referrals. Our team members feel valued, because they truly are. They go above and beyond the call of duty, to ensure we as a team achieve our goals and those of our clients.

Processes

When starting out, it's essential to work out your processes—that is, how the business should run. Ask yourself: What's important to me from a process perspective? What do I need to get right, and what do I want my processes to look like, to have the grand business I want to have within my three-year time frame? What processes do I want to have to make this the best business possible?

One of our goals at The Practice was to develop a seamless client experience. By that we meant that whenever our clients dealt with our organisation, it would be what we called 'admin resistant'. The processes in our business were client-centric—that is, they centred around the client's needs, not our needs.

I can't stand asking for something and being told, 'We don't do that here'. That's the last thing I wanted my business to be like. I'm constantly surprised to see 'No food or drink allowed' signs in small suburban shop windows—they must be doing fantastically to be able to turn away potential customers.

We didn't want our business to be location dependent or principal dependent, so we needed to have the processes in place so our business could achieve that. The first thing we did was invest heavily in our IT system: from servers and a back-up system to individual computers. We also moved to a 'paperless' office environment where everything is stored electronically. This robust IT system now allows us to work offsite, which is particularly important for the mums-to-be in the office — they will be able to work from home as part of their transition back into the workforce.

Also, we introduced client service managers (CSMs) whose role is to replace the partners (Rob and me) as the conduit of information between our clients and The Practice. This also allows us to focus more on providing strategic advice to clients and gives us time to work on the business (rather than just in it).

Customers

The next step is to work out what types of customers you want. At The Practice we knew we were building a business that was more than just an accounting practice. We wanted to offer an all-encompassing financial service, one that included wealth creation strategies and advice on tax-effective debt structuring. In other words, once the clients have made a profit, we wanted to advise them where to invest it through our financial planning arm and ensure the associated debt is structured in the most tax-effective way.

When we asked ourselves what the attributes of these ideal clients were, we decided that:

- they are interested in growth
- they have multiple advice needs
- they will be raving fans of our business and will refer like-minded clients to us
- they are going to be clients of The Practice, not of individual team members or partners, so should someone go on holiday or take maternity leave, that relationship will not be interrupted or at risk of causing us to lose that client
- they would be loyal to our brand.

A couple of strategies we introduced were:

- asking our existing 'A-category' clients to refer like-minded people to us

- altering our client-engagement process to ensure we explained, at the commencement of a new client relationship, what we do, how we do it, what we expect of the client and what the client should expect from us

- undertaking a client education program for existing clients, called 27 Steps to Achieving your Financial Goals, which explains the other services we offer (in addition to tax advice) that will help them achieve their financial goals.

It was only after we'd spent time brainstorming what we wanted our people, processes and customers to look like in three years' time that we had the information to identify what our financials would look like.

Financials

Financials are made up of a number of different elements. From a profit-and-loss perspective, financials include revenues and expenses—revenues minus expenses equals profit (or loss), with profit or loss being depicted in your balance sheet. Your people and processes drive your costs (expenses) and it's your customers that drive your income (revenue). So you need a clear understanding of what your people and processes should look like in order to predict your cost structures. Then you need to know what sort of customers you're trying to attract so you can see what your revenues should look like. From there, you can graph your targets for revenues, expenses, profitability, and, therefore, the value of your business—and why your brand is going to be so successful.

So for you current or future business owners out there, I recommend you adopt the balanced scorecard approach to help you achieve your business goals. Take time out of your business, so that you can work on it. Map out how you want your business to look in three years' time, broken down into people, processes, customers and financials. Then develop an action plan to help you get there. This process really works—The Practice is living proof! In 2007 we won the Small Business Champions award for Victoria.

The four secrets to business success

I strongly recommend anyone who is in business, or looking to start a business, follow these four simple steps to ensure your business is successful:

- develop a vision (using the balanced scorecard) — work out where it is that you're going

- create a mission statement — what you do, your purpose for being in business

- establish your core values or culture — what you believe in, how you do things

- know where you've come from — your history.

When Brad and Cindy came to me, they knew they wanted to start a business — they just didn't know how to go about it. By using the balanced scorecard management tool — focusing on the four business pillars, and developing a clear vision and mission statement — I worked with them to build a blueprint for the birth of their bouncing baby business.

I strongly recommend that anyone considering starting a business also uses these signposts to guide them in the right direction. Similarly, if you already have a business, use these tools as a road map to ensure you're on track for where you want your business to be.

Develop a vision

To be successful in business, you need a strong, united vision that everybody in the organisation is aware of. A vision is a clear picture of where you're going to be within a defined time frame.

At The Practice, we use the balanced scorecard approach to help form our vision. My partner, Rob, and I regularly revisit our vision: where do we see our business in the next three years? (You can use any period of time, from one to 10 years). Three years sounds like a long time, but it creeps up on you pretty quickly. We also prepare a 10-year vision to ensure we have a strategic long-term view of the business horizon.

Once we developed our vision, the first thing Rob and I did was to spend an evening with our team, to share our vision with them — where we were taking our business. Why? Because we're a team—without the buy-in of your team, your vision is just a bunch of words.

Create a mission statement

The next thing that's just as important as your vision is your mission statement. It defines what it is that you offer your clients; your purpose for being in business. What is it that you do? At The Practice, our mission statement is something that every team member knows and is proud of.

Now, I've seen plenty of mission statements in my dealings with clients, some 10 lines long, others half a page, that nobody is going to remember or understand. The theory is that to be effective and strong, a mission statement should be no more than 25 words. As an example, here's The Practice's mission statement: 'To help our clients achieve both their business and personal goals, through proactive service and ongoing advice'.

It's simple, to the point and explains the essence of what we do, and it's something that I'm passionate about living (not just putting up on the wall for show). If we can't live up to our mission statement, we don't take on an assignment.

I break that mission statement into four key areas:

1   We're focused on helping our clients.

2   Achieving their goals, both personal and business (not ours, but theirs).

3   We seek to provide proactive advice.

4   Developing an ongoing relationship with our clients.

A mission statement that has stuck with me over the years comes from my Ford days. It may have changed (it was over 11 years ago now), but at the time it read: 'To be the number one automotive producer in the world'. Mission statements as simple and concise as that can have a profound effect. The fact that I can remember it after all these years is proof of how powerful and memorable it was for me.

So ensure you have a strong, powerful mission statement that is easy to remember and describes exactly what you do, and make sure you believe in it. If you have a client or prospective customer that won't allow you to fulfil your mission statement, don't take on that client. From time to time, prospective clients come to us seeking one-off advice of a technical nature, with the intention of remaining with their existing accountant for all other matters. There's nothing wrong with this—we're experts in our field, so it makes sense, and I always respect loyalty. However, it goes against our charter of providing ongoing, proactive advice, so we have to decline these jobs.

Establish your core values

If your mission statement explains what it is that you do, you then need to define how it is that you do it. This becomes your core values or what we refer to as our culture.

Why is your culture so important? Because a business is nothing without its people. Crunch the numbers. Eight hours of sleep a day, plus three hours for breakfast, getting ready and commuting to and from work leaves your team members with 13 hours, of which you ask for eight. If you're asking your team members to be passionate about what they do for eight hours a day, then your role—nay, obligation—as owner or director or leader is to provide and cultivate an environment that not only encourages team members to be productive, but is also an environment that is enjoyable and conducive to your team members making the most of their valuable time. Sometimes business owners get confused and assume their employees owe them everything—well, they *don't*.

Like many of my clients, the hardest thing our business has found is how to attract and retain key people. So we developed our culture and core values, and also made one of our team members the director of culture at the firm. (Sounds a bit *1984*, I know, but we're more 'favourite uncle' than 'big brother'.)

The core values of The Practice are as follows:

- We care for our clients and team members.
- We work ethically and with integrity.
- We have fun while we're at work.
- We are committed and passionate about what we do.

I tell new clients that if we can't fulfil our mission statement or adhere to our core values, we won't take on the assignment. And I have sacked clients because my team members did not enjoy working on their file or were asked to do things that weren't ethical. So it's one thing to spruik that you have a vision, mission statement or core values, but another completely to live and breathe them.

Know where you've come from

The importance of being aware of your history was highlighted to me by Peter Cook, director of Love Your Business and a business coach for small to medium business owners (check out his website <www. loveyourbusiness.com>). Peter taught me the importance of knowing where you've come from—your story.

The first thing I did on hearing this advice was to contact a journalist friend of mine, Greg Clarke, and ask him to write our story. My partner and I, and our whole team, never forget that our business has come from humble beginnings. Where you've come from often shapes the culture within your organisation. My business partner and I have known each other since we were five, and we've gone from primary school to uni together. I met my wife through him. Then there were the early struggles as we fought to establish our business. These things are important, and shape how we operate now. Don't be defined by your history, but don't deny it or forget it either.

Diff'rent strokes

Despite the fact that all businesses have the four pillars in common, they all come in different shapes and sizes. To be successful in business, you don't necessarily have to be the biggest or the best. You simply need to ensure you have a *business*, rather than being self-employed. This is exemplified by the difference between a personal trainer and a gym owner. A personal trainer gets paid based solely on the number of hours he or she works—that is, you're self-employed. If you're sick, want to go on holidays, are getting married or having a baby, there's going to be a period where you can't work, therefore you're not going to get paid.

In contrast, the gym owner still gets paid regardless of whether he or she attends the gym or not (providing he or she has set it up correctly and has a good team in place). A male client of mine recently purchased a Fernwood gym franchise (a ladies-only gym), and one of the great things about this move is that he can't set foot in the place! He's forced to be a *true* business owner, and is required to use all his leadership skills to run that business remotely. He can't go in there and take a pump class (despite his sudden strong desire to don the lycra).

When I first started my business my focus was to be important enough so that my hourly rate could increase. At that time, The Practice's main source of income came from contracting to another accounting firm, where I was charging $27.50 per hour for my time. I now charge more than ten times that an hour. My next goal is to leverage my people's time so effectively that there's no reliance on me putting time in a time sheet.

You don't need to have organisations that employ 25 or 100 people to be seen as a business owner. For some, the cost of giving up our existing income and negotiating the barriers to starting a new business are too great. Remember, though, you can always have a job *and* a small or micro business that supplements your income. But to satisfy my definition of a business, the relationship or ratio between the time spent working on the business versus the return and reward needs to be significantly disproportionate.

These days, business can come in all shapes, sizes, and shades. One client of mine sells artwork online, while another owns not one but five Jim's Mowing franchises (he doesn't work in them himself, otherwise he'd be self-employed). Then there are the sweatshops—er, business ventures—run from home, like the one my mum and dad operated from the kitchen table (called micro businesses).

The internet presents boundless opportunities. Timothy Ferriss, in his book *The 4-Hour Workweek*, talks about the many opportunities to run internet-based businesses. There are numerous people who run businesses through eBay. Google and Yahoo! provide opportunities through search engines. The bottom line is everyone now has the opportunity to create their own little business.

Jay's take aways

- Business ownership is the ultimate form of leverage.

- Master the balanced scorecard reporting approach, where you report on all aspects of your business: your people, processes, customers and financials.

- Your people are your most important asset.

- Develop your processes so they support your people, and make them customer-centric.

- Work out who your ideal customers are.

- Only after you have established the other three pillars of business should you focus on your financials.

- Have a clear idea of where it is you're going (your vision).

- Be clear about why you're in business—what your purpose (your mission) is.

- Define what you stand for, and how you go about doing things (your core values).

- Remember where you came from (your history).

- Take time out of your business, so you can work on it.

- Understand the difference between owning a business and being self-employed.

- Always remember that business isn't easy. It takes hard work and persistence to establish a business, but the rewards are extraordinary.

- Businesses come in all shapes and sizes—these days, you can even run a successful, thriving business from the comfort of your own home.

Chapter 11

Protecting your ass(ets)

What you'll discover in this chapter:

ð   the importance of structuring the ownership of your assets correctly

ð   why you need to protect your assets

ð   the three steps to correct asset structure

ð   the difference between owning assets in your name, under a company and in a trust

ð   why you'll come to love self managed superannuation funds.

In this chapter I explain the different ways you can structure the ownership of your investment assets. Now, before you poke your eyes out with a pointy stick just to avoid reading such riveting subject matter, I urge you to stop and think:

▣   It'll hurt. A lot.

▣   The information I'm about to give you may come in very handy one day. Maybe not right now for you debt-busting Sarahs out there, but for anyone who owns significant assets, or plans to do so one day, this stuff could really save your bacon.

▣   If you own a business, or plan to at some stage, this stuff is pure gold dust.

You're about to get insights that would normally cost you a lot of cash. I can't believe I'm practically giving away this fantastic information. Lucky I like you.

If you own, run or operate a business, or you have some form of investment or personal asset(s), such as a property or shares, I'd almost slap you if you didn't have the appropriate ownership structure. There are three reasons for this:

- *asset protection* — so no-one can take them off you
- *flexibility* — so you can easily change your wealth creation plan to suit your changing needs
- *estate planning* — to ensure your assets go to the people you want them to if you fall off the twig.

You may be surprised to see there's not one reference to tax minimisation. You see, us accountants get a bad rap. Many people still think our main role is to work the loopholes so we can minimise the amount of tax our clients pay. Don't get me wrong, we wouldn't be doing our job right if we didn't advise our clients how to structure their affairs in a tax-effective manner, but the government deliberately introduced an anti-tax-avoidance provision to counteract such activity.

Instead, any good accountant will focus on the above three components. Tax savings are simply a by-product of getting these components right.

Asset protection

It's essential to protect our assets because, unfortunately, there are some bad people out there. Sneaky people. People who want to relieve us of our hard-earned cash. We have a hard enough time accumulating and building a portfolio without letting some bozo take it from us. And it pays to guard against us (or our employees) simply making a mistake.

Australia has followed the US and become a highly litigious society. Legal firms these days boast about their 'no result, no fee' service — so there are few barriers discouraging people from suing you. In a country that invented the tall poppy syndrome this spells trouble for anyone with something to lose.

These days, people don't want to take responsibility for their actions — it's easier to blame their misfortune on others and go after what they 'deserve'. So it's vital that your assets are protected from anyone who tries to sue you.

What's your likelihood of being sued?

The level of protection you need depends on how risk averse you are. Business owners in particular have a high risk of getting sued. Worse, it's not just *you* you have to worry about, but also employees who act on your behalf. Employees in their own right are also at risk — often a customer or client can hold them accountable. Employees can even be treated as shadow directors in some cases and thus be held liable.

Table 11.1 shows some of the businesses and jobs that are at risk of litigation. It's just a guide — the list is endless.

Table 11.1: Jay's risk-ter scale

Risk level	Businesses and jobs at risk of litigation
High	Business owners
	Security guards and businesses
	People selling goods or services to the public (including advice)
	Transport operators
	Truck drivers
	Accountants, financial planners, mortgage brokers
	Hospitality industry
	Medical practitioners, dentists and so on
Medium	Landlords — rental properties
	Employees in senior positions
	Providers of food
	Personal trainers
Low	Receptionists
	Factory workers
	Share traders (limited exposure to the public)

Where will it end? You may recall the spike in public liability insurance a few years ago, and the impact it had on hobbies and sporting clubs. The Practice's public indemnity insurance went up 250 per cent in one year!

What is asset protection?

I liken asset protection to a computer firewall. It creates layers of protection between you, your assets and the people who want to attack them. The aim is to be in a position where you can control your assets, but you don't actually *own* them—that way, no-one can claim them if they seek redress from you through the courts.

Monitor your behaviour

The first layer of asset protection is to monitor your behaviour and, for those of you in business, your team's behaviour. You need to implement quality assurance systems and processes to minimise the chance of anyone making a mistake. Most people don't deliberately set out to create problems, it's usually a case of not having clear instructions or guidelines to follow.

If appropriate, provide your clients with disclaimers—like I did at the start of this book! You see signs everywhere: Watch the step, Beware of the dog, HAZCHEM. All these are simple disclaimers, designed to ensure someone stupid enough to light a cigarette while filling up their tank with LPG can't claim he or she didn't know it was dangerous. These things are obvious to most of us, but today, you just about have to tie people's hands to prevent them stabbing themselves in the neck with your cutlery and claiming it was your fault.

There are hundreds of examples of crazy lawsuits—situations so bizarre they defy logic. After a lawsuit, Winnebago were forced to put a warning on the cruise control of their vehicles: Please beware that by engaging the cruise control, the car won't steer itself. Apparently some brainiac had expected the cruise control to turn corners for them.

In Texas a supermarket shopper successfully sued after injuring herself in the store. An out-of-control kid was running around and pulling food off shelves, which caused her to fall and break her ankle. Ironically, it was her child.

The chances of being sued are greater than they used to be; you need to watch your actions (and those of your employees) and install firewalls.

Get insurance

If you're in business, there are certain types of insurance you need to consider. It would be crazy for any business to not have public liability and professional indemnity insurance in place. You can also get directors' and officers' insurance to protect you as a director. Rental property owners should have public liability and landlords' insurance.

Simply having insurance doesn't solve all your problems, however. Insurance companies are very successful organisations—because they don't often lose. There may be times when you think you're covered, but you actually aren't. So read the fine print and beware.

Have the correct ownership structure of your assets

I'm a firm believer in separating your personal, business and investment assets. I don't want one to be affected by the others. If you operate your business through a company (company structures will be explained later this chapter), it would be crazy for that company to also own your share portfolio. This is because if the company was to be sued, they could take the company's assets—including your share portfolio.

However, before we get into the excitement of companies, trusts and other asset ownership vehicles, a common problem must be addressed. For most of us, our biggest asset is our family home. Anyone in business, or in a position where they may be sued, must structure their homeownership correctly. If someone sues you, they'll usually go for your biggest asset. The last thing anyone in business wants to do is put the family home at risk.

Following are three steps married readers can take (who are at risk of litigation and who own a property) to avoid this problem.

1   *Risk-taker, risk-averter.* Agree between yourselves to make one
     partner (generally the owner of the business) the risk-taker—
     the other becomes what I call the risk-averter. If you're setting

up a business, I'd recommend you make the risk-taker the sole director of the business, with the risk-averter being the sole owner of the family home. If anything goes wrong with the business, the house is safe.

2 *Resign the risk-averter as a director of the company.* Similarly, if you already have a business in place where you are both directors, remove the risk-averter as director so that the risk-taker is sole director.

3 *Transfer the risk-taker's share of the house to the risk-averter.* This is again to protect the family home from any business misadventure. It's a common strategy for couples that have purchased a house together, with the house being in both their names, to set up a business from which they will both earn an income. The risk-taker is made sole director of the business, and can then gift his or her share of the house to the risk-averter. Done correctly, you can avoid paying stamp duty and capital gains tax. The process involves the transfer of your interest in the property to your husband or wife in what's called 'fee simple' out of 'love and affection'. I strongly recommend you do this with a solicitor qualified in this area.

After what's called the clawback period (two years and six months), the property has no link to the risk-taker. If the risk-taker as director were to be sued, the main asset is not owned by him or her, so it can't be touched. But the safety of your house can't be guaranteed during that period.

Despite taking all these safeguards, you may still be sued. But once the third party suing you discovers that you don't have a house, a secondary benefit kicks in: the third party is unlikely to waste the time and money in litigation if he or she knows you don't have any assets in your own name. It can help avoid messy legal issues before they arise.

When I advise clients of this strategy, some of them cringe at the thought of surrendering ownership of their assets. They're obviously worried about the impact on them if the marriage ends down the track. Fair enough, too, as more and more marriages these days end in divorce. Male clients in particular are reluctant to take their name off the title—if they split, the wife will get everything. But as I tell them: if you get divorced, she'll get it all anyway!

In all seriousness, the family law court is the most powerful in the country. It's irrelevant who owns the house—whether behind a corporate veil, in one spouse's name or in joint names. The judge will determine how the assets are to be distributed in accordance with a host of factors.

If you're still nervous about taking your name off the title, there are alternatives to transferring full ownership:

- You can change ownership from joint names to tenants in common. The risk-taker owns 1 per cent of the house, and the risk-averter owns 99 per cent. This means the risk-averter can't sell the property without the other's consent. This gives some comfort to many nervous male clients of mine.

- Get a loved one or trusted confidant to take a debenture over your property, which is like a second mortgage. Thus there's no equity left for anyone to access. Two brothers I knew did this. Andy had a house worth $800 000, on which he owed $250 000 to the bank. His brother, Bill, registered a debenture for $550 000 (I would recommend this is done with your adviser and solicitor). If Andy ever needs to access the equity, he can ask his brother to remove the debenture. A great way to discourage litigation. Why doesn't everyone do it, I hear you ask? Well, it's hard to find a trusted confidant!

- Assign ownership of the house to a company or trust. I'll discuss this in more detail later in the chapter, but the downside is the home loses 'principal place of residence' status, and, as a consequence, you may lose CGT exemption upon the sale.

Types of asset structures

The reason ownership structure is so important is because the correct structure will provide you with asset protection, flexibility and estate planning. There are four structure types available:

- ownership in an individual's name

- company ownership

- trust ownership

- ownership using a self managed superannuation fund.

Ownership in an individual's name

Owning the asset in an individual's name, the most common strategy, provides minimal asset protection. You can use the strategies mentioned earlier to limit your exposure, but you have no flexibility. It does, however, provide a reasonable level of estate planning—as long as you have a will that is accommodating (this is discussed in more detail in chapter 12).

Company ownership

Ever wondered what Pty Ltd stands for? Proprietary Limited. The liability of the proprietors (the owners) to external creditors is limited, based on the paid-up capital of that company. 'Paid-up capital' basically means the 'paper' value of the company. You may have heard the term '$2 company'. Here, the company has two shares worth $1 each. Two shareholders contribute $2—the total paid-up capital of the company. The most someone suing you could get would be $2. Company ownership provides reasonable asset protection.

However, there are times when directors can be held personally liable, such as when they have signed a personal guarantee statement or have knowingly traded the company while insolvent. Also, there are certain circumstances where the Australian Taxation Office can hold you personally liable for the company's tax debts (but that's another book on its own).

A little about companies

As I mentioned in chapter 9, shareholders own companies. Directors run them.

A company and its owner(s) are two separate legal entities. Shareholders are owners—they have various rights such as the right to receive company profits in the form of dividends. They also have voting rights. Pty Ltd companies are similar to companies on the ASX. It's like people owning Telstra shares—they're 'owners', but they're not responsible for running the company. However, for most small businesses in Australia, the directors and shareholders are the same person or people.

One of the most exciting things about companies is the tax rate: a flat rate of 30¢ in the dollar. Whether you earn a profit of $1 or $550 million, the tax rate is the same. This differs for individuals, where we operate under the Robin Hood principle—the more you earn, the more tax you pay (as shown in table 11.2).

Table 11.2: marginal individual tax scale for 2009 financial year

Taxable income	Tax rate (%)*
$0 to $6000	0
$6001 to $34000	15
$34001 to $80000	30
$80001 to $180000	40
$180001 plus	45

*Note: you need to add the Medicare Levy (1.5 per cent)—so the top rate is actually 46.5 per cent.

As you can see, the maximum tax rate for individuals is 46.5 per cent—a significant difference from the 30 per cent company rate. Obviously, anyone looking to accumulate wealth would be wise to lower their tax rate if applicable.

Another feature of companies is their ability to accumulate profits—known as retained earnings. For example, a company could make $100000 profit, pay $30000 in tax and retain the $70000 for working capital in the company. It does not have to pay it all to the shareholders. Losses can also be carried forward into the future.

Jay's hot tip

I could carry on for another separate book on the benefits and workings of companies. But for the purposes of this book, I just want to give you an overview of some of the opportunities and pitfalls. Visit <www.wheresmymoney.com.au> for more business information.

Companies also provide a reasonable level of flexibility—more than an individual. They enable us to do various things such as employ and pay ourselves. They also enable us to employ a spouse and/or pay ourselves a dividend from any after-tax profits (if we were shareholders). Both the husband and wife can be shareholders and receive dividends, and can 'split' the income to potentially reduce their tax burden. Note that you can't pay dividends to one shareholder and not another—they must all receive a dividend if one is paid.

Despite its many advantages, company ownership is not as flexible as other structures. When splitting income between spouses through the payment of wages, you need to justify why the partner is receiving a wage and what the partner's role is.

Take the example of a husband and wife operating a landscape gardening business. The wife is a qualified landscape gardener and the husband does the books. During the year they made a profit of $200 000. It would be hard to argue they should both be on the same salary ($100 000) as they're not performing the same duties, and only one is providing income-generating services.

Remember that when you pay salary and wages in Australia, there are other on-costs to consider:

- you must contribute 9 per cent into superannuation for each employee

- you are liable for WorkCover (an insurance policy that employers must take out on the total remuneration paid to employees—salaries and super)

- state taxes, such as payroll tax (a personal favourite), are incurred if your wages bill is above a certain threshold.

Another limitation is that companies aren't as accommodating to the various capital gains tax discounts available in Australia, such as the 12-month discount and certain small business concession discounts.

Trust ownership

A trust has a similar legal status to a minor (not the Todd Russell and Brant Webb variety; I mean children). Minors can't really own assets—that is, you can't put assets in their name. However, their mother or father, as guardian, can own assets on their behalf. Therefore trusts require a guardian—or, in this case, a trustee—to act in its best interests. The role of a trustee is to administer the trust and make decisions on behalf of the trust.

There are four main types of trusts:

- discretionary (family)
- fixed (unit)
- hybrid
- other (including testamentary trusts and bare trusts).

Discretionary trusts

The most popular type of trust in Australia is a discretionary trust—commonly known as a family trust. Apart from the trustee, there are other important people in a discretionary trust:

- *appointor*. The appointor has the power to appoint or remove a trustee
- *settlor*. This is the accountant or lawyer who establishes the trust. To make it a legal document you need to contribute a settled sum (usually $10)
- *beneficiary*. There are three types of beneficiaries:
  - *primary*. For most family trusts, the primary beneficiaries are the husband and wife. You need to name your primary beneficiaries, but you don't need to then name secondary or tertiary beneficiaries
  - *secondary*. The secondary beneficiaries include children, brothers, sisters, aunties, uncles, grandparents—relatives of the primary beneficiaries
  - *tertiary*. The tertiary beneficiaries are companies or trusts (and, in certain circumstances, self managed super funds) that are owned or controlled by one of the primary beneficiaries.

One of the exciting things about trusts is they don't pay tax. The tax rate is 46.5 per cent for the top individual marginal tax rate, 30 per cent for a company, and 0 per cent for a trust. You read right: *zee-row*! The trustee, on behalf of the trust, distributes any profits to the beneficiaries, and it's those beneficiaries who subsequently pay the tax. So a trust allows us to legally split our income with other family members.

The trustee, at his or her discretion, chooses who will receive the income. Unlike a company paying wages to employees, and therefore needing to justify why the wage is paid, trusts have no such obligation. A trust can pay wages, so it can operate as a business and employ people. This also provides benefits such as tax-deductible superannuation contributions.

Take Brad and Cindy, for example, whose brilliant accountant advised them to structure the ownership of the business through a family trust. In their first year of business, Cindy stayed on at her previous employment and was earning a good wage. So there was no point distributing income from the business trust to her. The following year, she fell pregnant with their third child, and took 12 months off from paid employment. During that year, Brad distributed income to her from the business trust. When she went back to work on the same high income, Brad chose, at his discretion, not to distribute income to her.

Discretionary trusts are not limited to family members. They can be created by two people going into business together (primary beneficiaries); secondary beneficiaries would be any relatives of either primary beneficiary. But there is a risk that, if one of the business partners was the sole trustee, he or she could distribute all the profits to themselves.

Fixed trusts

The main difference between a fixed trust (commonly referred to as a unit trust) and a discretionary trust is that a fixed trust has a fixed entitlement — that is, the unit holders have a fixed entitlement to their share in the trust. This makes sense in some scenarios; for example, two people going into business together will usually set up a fixed trust with a fixed entitlement — 50–50, 60–40, 80–20 — whatever circumstances dictate.

Hybrid trusts

Hybrid trusts were flavour of the month a few years ago. Since then the tax office has clamped down on people using them inappropriately.

A hybrid trust is a combination of a fixed and discretionary trust. It provides fixed entitlements, as well as having a discretionary component. It's quite a flexible structure that allows you to not only distribute income to the fixed unit holders, but also to the beneficiaries on a discretionary level.

Other trusts

Other types of trusts include testamentary trusts and bare trusts. Testamentary trusts, which we look at in chapter 12, are used in wills as part of the estate-planning process. Bare trusts are less common and occur when one party (party A) holds an asset on behalf of another party (party B). Party A has no beneficial right to the asset and must exercise control on the instruction of party B.

Ownership using a self managed superannuation fund

Self managed super funds (SMSFs) are highly popular in Australia. At the time of writing, there are roughly 400 000 SMSFs in Australia. Crunch the numbers: there are 21 million people in Australia, of which less than half pay tax. These 400 000 SMSFs are owned by eight million people, which is quite a significant number of people (around 5 per cent of taxpayers) in control of their own super funds.

With an SMSF, your money is still in super, but rather than being in a superannuation trust run by someone else (such as an industry, retail or wholesale fund), it's your own fund.

The SMSF sector is highly regulated, as the government is aware that some people shouldn't really be trusted with looking after their own super. For example, SMSFs must be audited prior to lodging a tax return. Therefore, not only do you need to prepare financial statements and a tax return for your SMSF, it needs to be audited by an independent auditor prior to being lodged with the tax office.

Following are some of the rules governing SMSF's:

- An SMSF must have four or fewer members.

- All members must be trustees of the fund.

- Sole member funds also need another trustee (as there must be at least two trustees) or have a company to act as trustee. That second trustee does not need to be a member. The rule is all members need to be trustees, but all trustees don't have to be members.

- The sole purpose test applies to all SMSFs. The test is that the sole purpose of the super fund is to provide benefits to the members upon their retirement and no sooner—you can't access it until you retire. This means you can't roll your super money out of an industry or retail fund and into an SMSF, and then borrow money from your super fund. You can't use your SMSF to buy a car you drive to work. Your SMSF can, however, invest in antique cars that are going to appreciate.

- All super funds must have an investment strategy and need to outline the risk profile—what you're looking to invest in—to members. For example, your SMSF may invest 40 per cent in Australian shares, 30 per cent in cash and the remainder in international shares. You can make art or wine investments (such as Penfolds Grange). There is a range of other things you can and can't invest in—visit <www.ato.gov.au> or <www. thepractice.com.au> for more information.

There are two other exciting things about SMSFs:

- *the tax rate.* At just 15 per cent the tax rate is the best of any structure (except a trust). But once an SMSF enters pension phase—when you as a member are over 60 and decide to retire—the tax rate on the earnings of the fund, and when you take your money out of the fund, is zero. Trusts are also taxed at zero, but the beneficiary subsequently pays tax. An SMSF is a great way to accumulate wealth for your retirement and to build an asset portfolio that you will one day sell in retirement (with no capital gains tax).

- *asset protection.* Super is probably the most protected environment out there. The government wants to make sure we fund our own retirements, so it has put in place many regulations to ensure our savings are preserved.

Let's take a look at some examples of when you might use a particular structure and the tax advantages of each structure.

Example 1: Jack and Diane

Jack and Diane have three kids. They're doing the best they can. They own and operate a business together. Jack works in the business, while Diane works part time doing the books. She's also a stay-at-home mum. They both plan to derive an income from the business. This year's profit was $200 000.

They have three options:

- Jack can run the business in his own name. However, as we've seen, this provides no flexibility or asset protection, and the tax on the $200 000 profit is $70 000.

- They can operate the business through a company. This necessitates contributions for super and WorkCover to be made from the profits (let's assume the standard WorkCover rate of 2 per cent of remuneration—$4000—and super contributions of 9 per cent). Jack draws a wage of $150 000 and pays tax of $49 000; Diane draws a wage of $30 000 and pays tax of $4000.

- They can create a discretionary trust. As they are not required to prove their activities like a company, they can split the income evenly between them, so they both receive $90 000. The tax payable is now only $23 000 each (a total of $46 000). They can also distribute $1667 of unearned income tax-free to any minors (above this, the minor is liable to pay 66c in the dollar). Therefore, they can distribute $5000 tax free. Plus, as they're not paying wages, but instead distributing income, there are no WorkCover costs. The total tax paid will be $46 000.

Therefore, the most appropriate structure for operating the business, on many levels (but in this example, mostly for tax benefits), is through a discretionary trust. You can save $24 000 compared with an individual and $11 000 compared with a company. That alone is worth the price of this book!

Example 2: Zelda

Zelda is a single 35 year old who's not currently in a relationship, but one day hopes to find Mr Right and start a family. She has a positively geared investment (a share portfolio). She has a great job and earns a high income—she's on the top marginal tax rate (45 per cent).

As her income is more than sufficient to live off, she wants to reinvest the yield from this investment back into it and enjoy the benefits of compounding her return.

The best way for Zelda to own her investment is through a company, where her tax rate will be capped at 30 per cent. There are two ways she could do this. The first option is for her to set up the company where she is the sole shareholder; when she does get married, she can sell a portion of her shares to her husband so that they can split the dividends of the company (which reduces her tax burden). However, the sale of shares to her husband will incur capital gains tax, which reduces the attractiveness of the strategy.

The second option, which is the one I'd recommend, is for Zelda to set up a discretionary trust. The trust is the shareholder of the company, and Zelda is the trustee. When paying a dividend to the shareholders, the company actually pays it to the discretionary trust. Once Zelda is married and has kids, the trust can distribute dividends to her family members. But the real beauty of this strategy is that with the discretionary trust, Zelda can distribute some of the income to her husband without changing the ownership of the shareholding (unlike in the first option). She therefore avoids capital gains tax on the transaction, thus saving herself a big whack in tax.

(I honestly can't believe I'm giving this advice away for only $32.95. This stuff should be repaid in bullion, it's going to save you so much money!)

Example 3: Lewis

Lewis is gainfully employed and on a good wage. He's concerned about asset protection and potential litigation due to his line of work (he's a doctor). He wants to negatively gear an investment property.

There are many ways he can do this—two common methods are via a discretionary trust or via a fixed trust. In the first instance, Lewis can set up a discretionary trust, buy an investment property and put it in the name of a company in its capacity as trustee—the trust owns the property. He, in his capacity as director of the trustee, borrows money (effectively, the trust is borrowing the money). He tenants the property, so he receives rent. When you take out expenses such as depreciation, real estate agent expenses and interest, the property is being run at a loss.

Discretionary trusts can distribute profits to beneficiaries at the trustee's discretion. However, losses incurred by a trust are trapped inside the trust. Those losses need to be carried forward in the trust into the future until that trust begins to generate a profit. He can then offset the profit against losses that have been incurred. So the losses aren't 'lost', Lewis just may not get to benefit from them (tax wise) for a while.

Lewis would be better off purchasing the property using a fixed trust with a corporate trustee (the unit trust owns the property). He would then borrow money in his name to purchase units in the trust. The company, as trustee for the trust, owns the property (he doesn't own it); he owns units in the trust to the value of how much he borrowed.

The trust rents the property out, and pays all fees and costs associated to tenanting the property. The resultant net profit after depreciation (and there should be net profit) will be distributed to the unit holders (Lewis). He can offset that income against the interest expense that he's incurred on the loan. Thus, he has the ability to (a) negatively gear the property and (b) avail himself of an asset protection scenario—he does not actually own the property. Who says you can't have your cake and eat it too?

Example 4: Marlon

Marlon is 60, with five years until retirement. He's still gainfully employed, earns $120 000 a year and has a significant surplus income from his employment. He already has $800 000 in super and wants to contribute as much money to super as he can before retirement.

The best way for Marlon to do this is salary sacrifice as much disposable income as possible into superannuation, and use this as a vehicle to acquire assets that will appreciate, providing him with good capital growth. As Marlon is above 50, he can salary sacrifice up to $100 000 into super (as much as his cash flow permits) and take advantage of the 15 per cent tax rate.

And as he's 60, I'd advise Marlon to set up a TRAP—a transition to retirement strategy, which converts his existing super to a pension phase, where the tax on earnings and withdrawals is zero. The beauty of a TRAP is you can 'retire' but still work. So Marlon has $20 000 of salary to live off—if he needs more cash, he can withdraw it through the pension, tax-free! Marlon's gone from paying $40 000 tax on $120 000, to $2000 tax on $20 000. Gold!

Once Marlon's super balance has built up enough to allow him to stop working, he can officially retire. The money he was salary sacrificing into super can now also be converted into pension phase and enjoy a zero tax rate as well—that is, any capital gains incurred on the sale of the assets (such as selling shares or prestige cars), or any income those assets generate, will not be taxed.

Jay's take aways

- There are three reasons you need the appropriate ownership structure:

  - asset protection—so no-one can take your assets from you

  - flexibility—so you can easily change your wealth creation plan to suit your changing needs

  - estate planning—to ensure your assets go to the people you want them to if you die.

- Protect your assets in case you, your employees or business are sued.

- Create firewalls—layers of protection between you, your assets and the people who want to attack them. Control your assets, but don't own them.

- Monitor your, and your team's, behaviour through quality assurance systems, and use disclaimers.

- Get the right type and level of insurance.

- Have the correct ownership structure of your assets—seek professional advice. It can save you a lot of money and even deter potential litigation.

- There are four types of asset structures:

  - owning the asset in an individual's name (or a partnership of sorts)

- □ having a company own the asset
- □ having a trust own the asset (there are four main types of trusts)
- □ owning the asset using a self managed super fund.

- ◉ Trusts don't pay tax.
- ◉ The tax rate of SMSFs (15 per cent) is a great reason to create your own.

Chapter 12

Death and taxes

What you'll discover in this chapter:

- ☉   five ways to reduce your tax bill
- ☉   why you should maximise your super contributions
- ☉   how to take care of your assets (and your family) if you die prematurely or are injured
- ☉   the role of a testamentary trust
- ☉   the importance of having good advisers.

Let me say upfront—this chapter is dry, but I urge you to guts through it. It's gold, and will be well worth your effort—it's also the tenth step on your journey to financial prosperity. I guarantee it'll save you money somewhere along the way.

They say the only certainties in life are death and taxes. Both pretty boring, but important nonetheless. In this chapter we'll look at three boring but important topics:

- ▣   tax
- ▣   estate planning
- ▣   selecting advisers.

Once you use this information to help select your advisers, you will need to explore tax and estate planning with them in much greater detail, ensuring they are both tailored to your personal circumstances. But at least you'll do so armed with a basic knowledge of your options.

Tax

For most of us, tax is our biggest single outgoing along with our home loan or rent repayments. This alone should be an incentive to pay attention to the impact tax has on your spending. And in the last chapter, we saw the tax implications of different types of structures.

Now, I know what you're thinking: 'Yeah, yeah, you're an accountant—you *love* tax'. But that's not the case at all. Nobody likes paying tax. I'm not advocating tax avoidance, but in the words of a famous past Australian, Kerry Packer, 'I pay what I'm required to pay; not a penny more, not a penny less. If anybody in this country doesn't minimise their tax, they want their heads read because, as a government, I can tell you you're not spending it that well that we should be donating extra.'[1]

Based on Kerry's advice (and he knew a thing or two·about not paying a penny more tax than he had to), you would be negligent if you didn't maximise the deductions available to you.

So, how do you do it? I'm glad you asked.

Keep receipts

Be meticulous in keeping your receipts—all of them. I'm a big advocate of record keeping. It has so many benefits, including helping you create your budget and analyse your spending. But it also helps you prepare your tax return. In Australia we have a self-assessment tax system, where we determine the deductions we are going to claim. In the event of an audit you need to substantiate your claims, and to do that you need to keep your receipts. Rather than throw them in a shoebox, use a system—whether that be a filing system or a computerised record—to maintain all your receipts. It makes the preparation and lodgement of your tax return much easier, and you won't forget any potential claims that you could make.

---

1 K Packer, 1991, Senate Select Committee hearing into foreign media ownership, *Sydney Morning Herald*, 18 February 2006, p. 41.

Be on the front foot with your tax return

Make sure you've got an accountant (I tell you how, later in the chapter) who provides you with proactive advice. That means the accountant discusses tax planning strategies with you before the end of the financial year, so you can still make changes to benefit your tax situation.

Tax planning advice could include (depending on your situation) maximising your contributions into super; bringing forward certain expenses and delaying the receipt of income; prepaying interest on a rental property or share portfolio; participating in a tax effective investment; and restructuring the way your income is derived.

Take it upon yourself to understand what you can deduct

There are a number of resources available to help you understand which items you can deduct. These include:

- *The Master Tax Guide*, produced by CCH
- *The Taxpayers' Guide*, produced by Taxpayers Australia
- The Australian Taxation Office website <www.ato.gov.au>
- CPA Australia's website <www.cpaaustralia.com.au>
- The Practice's website <www.thepractice.com.au>.

But when assessing whether something can be claimed, remember the golden rule: there needs to be a nexus between the expense incurred and the revenue earned. A business trip may be claimable, but not the family holiday to Noosa.

There are hundreds of different deductions you can make — following are some of the most common:

- income protection insurance
- accounting or tax agent fees
- donations (to approved charitable organisations)
- certain self-education expenses
- motor vehicle expenses (where your car is used for work-related purposes)

- uniforms (and laundry of)
- union dues
- interest deductions against your investment income.

Invest in tax-effective vehicles

The main purpose of any investment should not be to get a tax deduction; that should really be your last goal. You should first consider return on investment (yield), capital growth potential and whether the investment is sound. Only then have a look at the tax consequences of the investment. But, where the other considerations allow, investing in tax-effective vehicles can be a good strategy.

Some tax-effective strategies include:

- negatively gearing an investment property
- margin lending or instalment gearing into a direct share portfolio or managed investment
- investing in certain agribusiness investments that provide an annuity-style income (this, in particular, is not an investment that suits everyone—it's more for those on the top marginal tax rate; speak to your financial adviser before jumping in)
- investing in structured investment products and pre-paying the interest in a financial year.
- maximising your contributions into superannuation. This is really important and a great way to make tax savings. I can't think of too many Australians who wouldn't benefit from maximising the potential that exists inside super.

Maximise your contributions into superannuation

I touched on super in the previous chapter when I introduced self managed super funds (SMSFs). Everybody should maximise their contributions into super, however—not just those with an SMSF. The government provides so many incentives for us to contribute to super. I could fill another book with the ins and outs of super, so here are just a few points everyone should consider.

Firstly, the tax rate. If you're on the top marginal tax rate, you can make contributions into super and only pay 15 per cent tax, rather than 46.5 per cent—that's nearly 70 per cent less! Even if you're on an average wage and paying 30¢ in the dollar, the tax rate is still halved. And don't forget, once you go to pension phase, the tax rate drops to zero.

Secondly, the government has introduced the co-contributions scheme for lower income earners. For every one after-tax dollar you contribute to your super, the government will match it with $1.50 (up to a maximum of $1500 dollars). For example, if you earn less than $30 000 and you contribute $1000 of after tax money, the government will see you and raise you $500, meaning you get an extra $1500— tax-free—towards your retirement.

Finally, not only does super provide a tax benefit, it also reinforces one of my previous points—you can't spend what you don't have. By making extra contributions to super, you're reducing the likelihood of spending your cash on wants. Instead, you can sleep safe in the knowledge your surplus cash is working to give you the best lifestyle in retirement.

Estate planning

Estate planning helps you ensure your affairs will be more manageable if you die or become incapacitated. While ownership of any assets held jointly will revert to the survivor, most other assets form part of your estate. In the absence of a will, you will be deemed to have died 'intestate' and your assets will be distributed in accordance with the relevant government legislation.

For example, at the time of writing, Victorian intestacy laws state that if you have a spouse and child(ren), your spouse will receive the first $100 000 of your estate plus one-third of any balance. The remaining two-thirds will be held in trust for your child or children equally. As this may result in an unintentional outcome (for example, an estranged but not divorced spouse gets money you hadn't intended him or her to), I don't recommend you rely on these provisions. Rather, you should consider your circumstances very carefully and ensure you put in place a will that provides for your wishes regarding the distribution of your estate.

If you die without a will, the statutory distribution of your assets may be contested by your family and/or friends, and have to be resolved by the courts (although this can happen even if you have a will, but it's less likely). This is yucky town. A good way to tear a family apart is to get them fighting over money. I see this as one of the drawbacks of DIY will kits. I'm a big advocate of understanding your situation, then discussing it with a solicitor, and drawing up a will that meets all your goals and intentions for when you pass away.

The other component of estate planning is in the event you become incapacitated. If you become totally and permanently disabled, your assets may be frozen if no-one has the authority to act on your behalf. Your family may have to meet any medical expenses or other costs as they would not be legally allowed to access your finances to help pay for them.

Given these two issues, as a minimum everybody should do the following:

- Have your will drawn up and review it every five years and/or during periods of significant change to either your position or your personal situation. For example, if you get divorced or remarried, or go into business.

- Implement an enduring power of attorney. This ensures your wishes are carried out without the need to gain approval from the relevant government authority. This is perfect if you're either absent (for example, overseas) or incapacitated and unable to act on your own behalf due to circumstances (such as through illness or accident). Obviously, you need to appoint this enduring power of attorney before you become incapacitated.

- Appoint an executor (not someone who executes people—it's pronounced 'exek-you-tor') of your will in the event you fall off the twig. The conditions and terms outlined in your will need to be administered by somebody upon your death. This person is referred to as an executor (or executrix if female—but don't worry, there's no leather or chains involved). The executor is usually your spouse or another family member, a close friend, or a solicitor or accountant. You can also appoint co-executors.

  As the position holds a large amount of responsibility and can be complex, it's important that you discuss your wishes with the person prior to nominating him or her executor in your will. This person has the right to accept or decline your appointment.

The duties of an executor include arranging the funeral, applying for probate, paying all outstanding debts including tax (the executor becomes personally liable for the payment of any tax due in respect of the deceased's tax return), keeping appropriate records for CGT purposes, and may need to act as trustee of a testamentary trust should that be set up.

The executor will also need to prepare and lodge a deceased estates tax return, from the date of death until June 30 (so the deceased effectively lodges two tax returns in the one financial year—one for the period while alive, the other is a deceased estate tax return). As a deceased estate can actually exist for three years for tax purposes, the executor will also need to lodge any subsequent returns. So while winding down (selling) the assets of the estate, you may need to lodge three returns, one a year.

If a husband and wife are executors for each other, it pays to have another executor if the unthinkable happens and you both pass away at the same time. It's also advisable to appoint someone who's not likely to drop off before you do, so avoid nominating your parents.

- You may consider including a testamentary clause in your will, which creates a testamentary trust for investments upon your death. This is simply a discretionary trust that is directed to be set up under a will. It provides your family with a range of additional benefits not normally associated with a standard will. It effectively gives you powers from the grave (not zombie-style, fortunately—though we'd all love to terrorise a mean boss or an ex). Testamentary clauses are used in situations where you want to leave money for your kids; the money can be left in a testamentary trust.

Let's say the executor invested $1 million in a mixture of cash and a share portfolio that generated 10 per cent per annum. If invested in a testamentary trust, you can distribute that income to the kids. Normally, the maximum unearned income minors can receive before paying tax is $1667. Anything above that is taxed at 66 per cent. The main benefit of this trust is that it allows distributions to minors to be treated at adult tax rates—a massive opportunity. The first $6000 is tax free. If you add in the low-income earner's rebate, you now have $11 000 tax free. Obviously, only the assets that are part of this estate can be included in this trust. For the latest tax rates, visit <www.thepractice.com.au>.

A testamentary clause can also shield a beneficiary's entitlement from creditors. You're not giving the money physically to the beneficiary; it's sitting in the trust. You can nominate how much to distribute to your children. For example, if you have young children, you can give them, say, $20 000 per year, and when they turn 21 give them access to the capital.

Other benefits include protecting pension entitlements of spouses and relieving certain beneficiaries from asset management responsibilities; for example, if your beneficiaries are minors or elderly, incapacitated, or not financially astute, you then leave it to the executor to administer the trust and make distributions as you see fit.

◉ If you're married, appoint your spouse as your binding death nomination within your superannuation. In the event of your death, your super will revert to your binding death nominee, so it bypasses the estate planning process (probate and will) and gives your spouse access to it straightaway.

There are two reasons you should do this. First, the estate and probate process can take a long time, so appointing your spouse as your binding death nominee gives him or her quick and easy access to money. Thus, there's some breathing space before any assets need to be sold. Second, it's a tax-effective way to distribute your super; if paid to a dependent, it's tax-free.

Review your binding death nomination periodically, or at a minimum every three years.

Selecting advisers

Selecting advisers (or surrounding yourself with good people) is something I firmly believe in. If you pay peanuts, you get monkeys. Also, I'm a professional myself, and I practise what I preach.

When my wife fell pregnant with twins, we were ecstatic. This turned to horror when we were told they had twin-to-twin transfusion syndrome, meaning one child gets too much of the blood supply, while the other doesn't get enough. We were told that in two weeks, the smaller twin (now our healthy son, Lewis) would 'demise'.

We immediately got a reference to an expert in multiple, complicated births: Dr Mark Umstad. A leader in his field, Dr Umstad looks, acts and charges like a professional. The end result is that our boys are, six years later, happy and healthy—and I attribute a large part of that to the professional, expert work done by Dr Umstad and his team.

Similarly, to make it financially, you need to have the following professionals at your disposal (and they need to be good at their trade):

- an accountant or a tax adviser

- a financial planner

- a mortgage or finance broker

- a lawyer or solicitor.

The activities of all four are interrelated, so they need to communicate with each other and all be kept in the loop. When buying a house, you need a good mortgage broker to get the right loan. He or she needs to liaise with your accountant to ensure the loan is structured correctly. Conveyancing needs to be done by your solicitor.

Similarly, when your financial planner discusses estate planning with you, such as life and TPD insurance, he or she will recommend you speak to a solicitor to ensure you put the appropriate will and powers of attorney in place.

You also need to ensure these professionals are right for you, and vice versa. The greatest tax barristers in the land might charge $900 an hour, but they're not the right adviser for the average punter. At The Practice, we enter into a commitment statement with new clients—we interview them to ensure they will be a good fit for our firm and we ask that they interview us to ensure that we're a good fit for them. It's important that the client and service provider are on the same page right from the start of the relationship.

Tips to help you choose your advisers

Here are some things you can do to help you choose the right advisers:

- Check that the firm you choose is affiliated with, and a member of, the relevant governing body. This helps ensure the firm conducts itself professionally at all times, and keeps abreast of the latest best-practice activities. For example, accountants should be members of CPA Australia or the Institute of Chartered Accountants, financial planners should be members of the Financial Planning Association, mortgage brokers should be members of the Mortgage & Finance Association of Australia and lawyers are registered regardless.

- Make sure you can relate to your adviser. It's important that you can have a business relationship. The key to business, I've found, is communication. If you cannot communicate effectively and efficiently with your adviser, you'll never get anywhere.

- Ask friends. Word-of-mouth referrals from trusted sources are tough to beat.

- Conduct an initial interview. Ask the advisers questions and let them find out about you. Now is a good time to get them to prove what they would do in certain situations: if faced with a certain event, what would they advise? This can give you comfort that they're a good fit for you.

- Make sure the advisers are transparent with how they charge. Don't do this just to shop around for the best price—you shouldn't choose an adviser just on price alone. Ask them what and how they charge so you're fully aware of how much dealing with them is going to cost.

Jay's hot tip

I'm a bit biased, but the first adviser you should source is an accountant. Everyone needs one. You might not need a solicitor—at least until you purchase a house or something similar.

Jay's take aways

- Tax is our biggest single outgoing along with our home loan or rent repayments. You can reduce your tax bill by:

  - keeping receipts

  - being proactive with your tax return

  - getting good professional advice

  - learning what you can deduct ·

  - investigating tax-effective investments.

- Maximise your contributions into super. There are several great incentives to do this:

  - the tax rate is 15 per cent (zero at pension phase)

  - the co-contributions scheme for lower income earners

  - it's forced saving—can't spend what you don't have.

- Set up a will to ensure your affairs are taken care of properly if you die or become incapacitated. Most of your assets (not owned jointly) form part of your estate. Make sure you:

  - have your will drawn up and review it regularly (for example, every five years)

  - implement an enduring power of attorney

  - appoint an executor of your will

  - consider including a testamentary clause in your will, which creates a testamentary trust for investments upon your death

  - create a binding death nomination for superannuation.

- Get a trusted team of professionals behind you, including:

  - an accountant or a tax adviser

  - a financial planner

  - a mortgage or finance broker

  - a lawyer or solicitor.

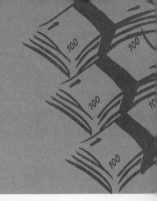

Chapter 13

Ten steps to financial freedom

What you'll discover in this chapter:

ŏ   this is where you ride off into your bright new financially astute sunset ...

Okay, it's time to put everything you've read into action. It's true that knowledge is power, but often what separates the haves from the have-nots is putting that knowledge into action. A marathon begins with a single step—so get started.

I honestly believe that anyone can achieve financial prosperity—provided you listen to me and follow this 10-step action plan. I'm passionate and pumped about it! (Where appropriate, I've included tools on my website <www.wheresmymoney.com.au> to make your journey that much easier.)

It doesn't matter where you are on your financial journey, you'll still gain an enormous benefit from these 10 steps. The case studies are proof of this.

Here they are, my 10 steps to moneytown:

1   Get your head right.

2   Understand your risk profile and protect yourself.

3   Consolidate bad debt.

4   Create a budget.

5   Maximise your income-earning potential.

6   Buy property — the smart way.

7   Have a crack at the sharemarket.

8   Business — the ultimate in leverage.

9   Protect your assets.

10   Get some help from the tax man.

Let's take a closer look at each of them.

Step 1: get your head right

Before embarking on your journey to financial prosperity, you need to get your head right. This means understanding the difference between needs and wants, and the relationship with that typical Aussie trait of spending what we earn — keeping up with the Joneses. This may be why you're not where you want to be financially. So you need to change that mindset and develop what I referred to in chapter 1 as a 'wealthy' attitude.

It's important to reprogram your psyche and know where you're going — so you can start with the end in mind. It's best to write down your goals, so that you can visualise what it is you want to achieve. I have friends who use a 'vision board', which is a collage of pictures and words that represent their goals. They hang it in their living room so that every day they reinforce where they want to be, so in their mind it becomes a reality — the first step! They update it every year to keep it accurate. If using a vision board seems a little extreme for you, you might just prefer to list your goals in a journal.

But doing the vision board obviously works for them — they've become the world's fittest couple! The authors of *Change Your Body with the World's Fittest Couple* (check it out — it's a great read), Matt and Monica, are living proof that with the right mindset, you can achieve anything.

To recap, the first step is to list your goals. Write them down, cut out a picture of your dream home and stick it on your vision board—whatever it takes to document them. Then put clear time frames on achieving these goals.

Step 2: understand your risk profile and protect yourself

Simply understanding the associated risks of investing (and not investing!) can have a profoundly positive effect on you and help you become a better investor. You understand the markets a little better, and that fluctuations happen in normal market conditions; you'll then become more patient about your investment's performance.

The single biggest financial risk facing most Australians is the risk of being underinsured and/or having the wrong type of cover. In times of unprecedented levels of debt it is irresponsible and financial suicide to be underinsured. The different types of cover were outlined in chapter 2. You can use the tools at <www.wheresmymoney.com.au> to work out what the right level of cover is for you, and how to structure that cover in the most tax-effective manner.

Step 3: consolidate bad debt

As you saw with the trouble young Sarah got herself into, bad debt (such as credit cards, personal loans and short-term finance) can be like a noose around your neck. With interest rates for credit cards almost three times that of home loan rates, it often compounds into nothing short of a financial disaster. If you find yourself in such a position, do everything in your power to get rid of that debt and never get yourself into that situation again.

As discussed in chapter 3, credit cards can be good tools if used correctly; for example, if they're paid off every month and if you have the discipline to spend within your means. If you decide to buy something from a store over an interest-free period, ensure that your repayments will pay off the item within the interest-free term.

Step 4: create a budget

Every successful business revisits its budget annually. So too do federal and state governments. I know it's boring and methodical, but it's absolutely critical to your financial success—it's the linchpin of all successful wealth creation plans. Without it, achieving financial freedom is just pot luck.

Remember the three components for a successful outcome with your family budget (which we covered in chapter 4). Sit down (with your significant other, if applicable) and work out what your goals are—what it is that you're saving for. Then create your budget using last year's income and expenditure, adjusted for any changes. Finally, link it to your asset and liability statement.

The golden rule is *bottom-up budgeting*—let profit drive the outcome. Chances are, after your first cut, the budget you've designed won't deliver the desired outcome you were looking for. So go back and rework the numbers, reduce your expenditure where possible (using the tips highlighted in chapter 4) to ensure you achieve the level of net disposable income (NDI) that will help you achieve your goals within your desired time frame.

Step 5: maximise your income-earning potential

The budget-creation process should have opened your eyes to many things—not least of which the enormous potential to increase your NDI. After exhausting all the avenues of expense reduction in step 4, the opportunity now exists for you to address the other half of the equation—your income.

Don't be satisfied with your current income level. Speak to your boss to let him or her know that you want to excel at work—you want more from your job and you'd like to know what you could do to get a promotion (and subsequent pay rise). If the boss isn't too accommodating, perhaps that organisation isn't right for you. It may simply be time to move on and sell yourself to a more like-minded company.

If the desire to achieve your goal is strong enough, like it was for my parents when I was growing up, you have other options. Perhaps a second job is in order or perhaps a small business from home. It didn't hurt my parents or our family; on the contrary, it got my parents back on track in an accelerated time frame and inadvertently provided us kids with the discipline and the belief that if we wanted to, we could achieve anything! (Even write a book!)

Step 6: buy property — the smart way

Not only do I believe that you can buy a property in your working life, I firmly believe you can buy (and keep) *two*! All you have to do is follow the principles set out in this book, and you can do it. Remember, Rome wasn't built in a day, so there's no need to have a multimillion-dollar property portfolio by the time you're 40. Most of you will agree that two houses is pretty good.

As I explained in chapters 6 and 7, how you structure your property purchase is crucial to ensuring you minimise the interest you pay on your loans, while also maximising any tax benefits you may be eligible for. And using the tools outlined in chapter 8, ensure you're armed with the information to beat the banks at their own game.

Step 7: have a crack at the sharemarket

Who said the sharemarket isn't for you? Not me, that's for sure. There are many myths about the sharemarket that just aren't true. A lot of people are frightened by the market because they don't understand it and generally any media attention is negative. It's doom and gloom that sells newspapers.

What I can tell you, though, is that over the long term, the sharemarket offers a lot of good news. Take the example I highlighted in chapter 9: if you invested $10 000 in June 1987 in the All Ordinaries Accumulation Index fund, in 2008 it would have been worth $80 000! Pretty impressive return, huh? And that's after some significant global events did their best to hammer the market: the tech wreck in 2000, the September 11 terrorist attack and the Bali bombings, the invasion of Kuwait and the war in Iraq. Despite these traumatic events, the Australian sharemarket still managed to increase eight-fold in 20 years.

If your investment horizon is five years or longer, do yourself a favour and take advantage of this wonderful opportunity to diversify your investment portfolio and participate in the market. It's best to do this with a professional who can guide and advise you on this journey.

Step 8: business—the ultimate in leverage

Of my 10 steps to financial freedom, step 8 is the only one that isn't compulsory. You see, business just isn't for everyone; us business owners are a different breed (I often get told I'm 'not normal'—I assume it's because I own a business...).

For those of you in business (or contemplating the leap one day), there are four integral things you need to focus on and get right (which we covered in chapter 10):

- your mission statement—your purpose for being in business
- your core values—what you as a team believe in
- a vision of where you see your business in the future
- an action (business) plan to help you achieve that vision.

The best way to do these is using the balanced scorecard approach to business development, which addresses the four pillars of your business: your people, your processes, your customers and your financials.

Step 9: protect your assets

We have a hard enough time accumulating wealth without having to worry about the threat of someone trying to take it from us. Make sure you put as many firewalls around your assets as possible so they are protected from attack and litigation.

Start by monitoring your behaviour; there's no need to attract attention to yourself. For those in business, ensure that you've implemented the appropriate quality assurance systems to reduce the chances of error and mishap that may lead to client dissatisfaction and subsequent litigation.

Secondly, make sure you've got the appropriate levels of insurance cover, from public liability to professional indemnity, and for property owners, landlords' insurance.

Finally, the ownership structure of your assets is critical. Make sure you own nothing, but control everything. As I mentioned in chapter 11, it's never too late to be structured correctly.

Step 10: get some help from the tax man

I know they're boring, but tax, estate planning and having a team of advisers are important! Surround yourself with a group of profess-ionals who you feel comfortable with and you can trust, and don't be frightened to pay for professional advice. Think of it this way: if you were incorrectly charged with an offence and facing life in prison, would you want the best lawyer in the land representing you, or the cheapest? I know which one I'd want—just like my wife and I did with our obstetrician for the twins.

The key people who can assist you on your journey are:

- an accountant—to advise you on tax and the structuring of your assets, and to provide general business advice

- a financial planner—to assist with your wealth creation plan and risk management strategy

- a mortgage or finance broker—to help you source the most appropriate and tax-effective loan for your circumstances

- a lawyer—to assist with your estate planning needs and the conveyancing requirements of your property portfolio.

Finally, educate yourself as much as possible—education is the key—ignorance is not a defence in law, nor can you rely on it in retirement. Use this book as a stepping stone on your journey to financial freedom. Also, take advantage of the tools on my website. The time to take control of your own destiny is now. *If it's to be, it's up to me.* You can do it!

Good luck!

JC

Glossary

asset something owned by a person or company that can be converted into cash. An asset can be tangible (machinery or a house) or intangible (goodwill).

Australian Securities Exchange (ASX) the main stock exchange in Australia. Formerly the Australian Stock Exchange, it was renamed in 2006 after merging with the Sydney Futures Exchange.

All Ordinaries Accumulation Index a measure of the change in stock prices of companies listed on the All Ordinaries Index.

All Ordinaries Index also known as the All Ords, the index comprises the 500 largest companies listed on the ASX by market capitalisation.

bear market a period of negative expectations about the performance of stock prices. Investors often sell in anticipation of losses, which can exacerbate the downward pressure on prices and fuel negative sentiment.

blue-chip stock a safe, financially stable, reliable, large company (commonly those in the top 20 on the ASX).

bull market a period of increasing investor confidence, where investors buy with the expectation of future price increases.

capital gains tax (CGT) tax on the profit from the sale of an asset such as an investment property, business or shares.

compound interest occurs when accumulated interest is added back to the principal (that is, the interest becomes compounded).

consumer price index (CPI) a government-calculated index used to determine the level of inflation. It is a measure of the average price of consumer goods and services purchased by households.

debt shifting the practice of illegally converting non-tax-deductible debt (for example, debt associated with your principal place of residence) into tax-deductible debt.

deposit down payment on the acquisition of an investment or any type of good or service. Also refers to an amount placed into a banking institution.

directors' and officers' insurance an insurance policy that protects the personal assets of directors and officers against any claim as a result of a 'wrongful act' committed by them in the course of doing their job.

direct shares an investment in a company or companies listed on the ASX, as opposed to an investment in a company or companies via a managed fund.

discount broker unlike a traditional broker, where advice is sought and given, discount brokers are used only to make a trade (generally online trades).

disposable income your gross income less income tax on that income.

diversification a form of risk management whereby a wide variety of asset classes are held within an investment portfolio.

dividends payments made by a company to its shareholders. Companies often retain some profits and pay the rest as a dividend.

equity the value of an asset (a property or business) less the associated liabilities of owning that asset.

folding money in note form.

franked dividends payments to shareholders on which the company has already paid tax. Franked dividends have imputation credits attached to them, which entitle investors to a rebate for tax already paid.

full-service broker offers a range of services to clients (such as advice on investments; investment plans; and planning, implementing and monitoring of your investment portfolio) and provides a personal point of contact.

fully financed business assets, such as equipment or motor vehicles, that have been 100 per cent financed (that is, no cash reserves have been used) using hire purchase, lease or chattel mortgage.

fundamental analysis the use of past and present information (such as financial statements, management structure, competitors and markets) to make financial forecasts.

imputation credit *see* franked dividends.

income-producing asset an asset that produces a return (yield) such as shares, property and business. These differ from non-income-producing assets such as your home (dwelling) and luxury items (caravan, plasma TV).

instalment gearing an investment strategy where you invest in managed funds on a monthly basis using a combination of your own money and funds borrowed from a lending institution, with the investment used as security.

landlords' insurance an insurance policy designed for rental property owners to cover all aspects of property ownership including accidental damage, public liability, loss of rent, rent default and loss of building value.

large thousand; usually referring to dollars.

lay-by a method of buying goods (particularly popular in the 1970s and 1980s) where an item is placed on hold until the purchaser has paid it off.

lenders mortgage insurance (LMI) an insurance premium, generally payable by the borrower, which covers the lender against non-payment or default on a property loan. It is a one-off fee that can vary according to the amount borrowed and size of your loan. If you have less than a 20 per cent deposit when purchasing a property, you may be liable for LMI.

liquidity   the ability to convert a share into cash easily through buying and selling, without causing a significant impact on its price and therefore value. Shares that make up the ASX top 20 are highly liquid (that is, there are many buyers and sellers).

listed property trusts   a large portfolio of properties, which due to their size and value are generally out of reach of the average investor. These large investments are broken up into smaller pieces called units that can be purchased by investors.

loan to value ratio (LVR)   an amount lent in relation to the value of a security. For example, an LVR of 70 per cent means you must contribute 30 per cent of your own funds to purchase the security.

long trading   this implies a bullish view of the market and refers to when a trader purchases an instrument to initiate a transaction. When buying shares, traders have a long view of the market. Also referred to as long or going long.

managed funds   made up of a pool of money that allows investors with similar goals to individually invest in a fund. Also referred to as managed investment schemes, managed investments or unit trusts, and are managed by professionals.

margin call   investors who borrow to purchase shares may receive a margin call if the value of the share portfolio falls below the lender's acceptable LVR level, often around 80 per cent. A margin call requires the investor to repay the loan to bring the LVR back to an acceptable level, normally 70 per cent.

market capitalisation   the market assessment of a company's value. Calculated by multiplying the total number of shares on issue by the current share price.

negative gearing   a form of leverage where an investor borrows money to buy an asset (usually property or shares), but where the income generated from the asset does not cover the expenses such as the interest on the loan. The resultant loss can help offset your overall tax liability.

net disposable income   your disposable income less your household expenditure.

online broker   a simple execution platform used by investors or traders. This platform may be either web based or an application that is installed on an investor's computer. The application allows people to place orders directly into the market without using a human broker.

pineapple   Australian colloquial term for a $50 note.

price–earnings ratio (P/E ratio)   the price paid for a share divided by the annual earnings per share. The higher the P/E ratio, the more you pay for each unit of income.

professional indemnity insurance   generally provided to professionals in the service sector to cover them against potential claims and civil liability. Cover is tailored to their specific industry for advice given and personal or other damage they may cause.

public liability insurance   insurance up to a stated limit for when you become legally liable for personal injury, including death, or damage to property, as a result of an occurrence connected with your business (or investment property in certain circumstances).

redraw facility   a facility within certain types of home loans where the bank or financier allows you to access the equity in your property (up to a pre-approved limit).

residual amount   the amount you have to pay to own a vehicle at the end of the lease term.

Rule of 72   an economic principal that summarises the compound effect of investing in shares. If an investment generates a return of 7.2 per cent per annum, and you reinvest that return back into the investment each year, the Rule of 72 states that your portfolio will double every 10 years. To calculate the number of years it will take for an investment to double, divide 72 by the anticipated return on that investment.

S&P/ASX 200 index   an index made up of the top 200 shares in the ASX.

separately managed accounts (SMAs)   provide all the benefits of investing in the sharemarket, namely into targeted asset classes, with the added benefit of the portfolio being professionally managed. Brokerage rates are low as they are conducted at wholesale rates.

serviceability   when assessing whether to lend money to a borrower, lending institutions usually review your last two years of income to determine your serviceability—that is, your ability to repay the loan.

share portfolio a person who owns shares in a number of companies has a 'portfolio'. This provides the investor ownership in part of a company which gives him or her certain rights such as the right to participate in profits through dividends, voting rights and, in the event the company is dissolved, the right to a claim against assets remaining after all debts have been paid.

short trading this implies a bearish view of the market and refers to when a trader sells shares with a view to purchasing them at a later date and a lower price to generate substantial profits. Tools such as contracts for difference (CFDs) can be used to short sell. Also know as short or going short.

structured products capital-protected investment portfolios, generally with a term of five years.

superannuation contribution employers are required to make superannuation contributions on behalf of most employees. The levy is 9 per cent and may be supplemented by a smaller compulsory contribution by the employee.

T+3 when buying or selling financial products, such as shares in a listed company, the title or legal ownership of those financial products must be exchanged for money. This exchange is called settlement and takes place three business days (T+3) after the buyer and seller agree to trade.

technical analysis the use of price and volume action on a share chart to reach conclusions about the likely direction of future price activity.

volatility the degree of fluctuations in an investment—for example, share prices, exchange rates or interest rates. Generally, the higher the volatility, the riskier the security.

yield the return on an investment expressed as a percentage.

Index

Get online and get ahead!

You've taken the first step to a new financial you by reading *Where's My Money?* Now fast-track your prosperity by visiting <www.wheresmymoney.com.au>. You'll find a host of tools, tips and teachings to help you on your journey, including:

- expert advice on money management strategies

- home loan and insurance calculators

- worksheets, including budget templates, and asset and liability statement templates

- online finance forums discussing a range of topics

- links to other recommended websites

- free membership—join up now and receive Jay's regular newsletter.

You can also book Jay for an exciting, fun-filled, passionate presentation on Where's My Money?

the PRACTICE
A Fresh Approach To Your Financial Solution

At The Practice, we do things a little differently. It starts with the relaxed, friendly attitude and the comfortable environment we create. You may even find yourself having fun!

We don't just focus on achieving the best possible outcome for you; we work with you to develop a strategy together, and regularly keep you informed of its progress. We go to great lengths to understand your personal and business objectives, and we're committed to meeting your needs with professional ongoing advice and proactive service.

Our friendly team specialises in a diverse range of areas, giving you the best outcome possible in:

- Taxation
- Accounting
- Asset Protection
- Business Consulting
- Wealth Management
- Risk Management
- Lending Solutions.

Once you're a client of ours, you can relax knowing your financial future is in expert hands.

If you're ready to start making real, lasting changes to your financial situation, come and see us at The Practice.

(03)8888-4000
www.thepractice.com.au

wealth management

finance solutions

accounting